Nicklaus by Design

Nicklaus by Design

GOLF COURSE STRATEGY AND ARCHITECTURE

BY JACK NICKLAUS WITH CHRIS MILLARD   FOREWORD BY PETE DYE

HARRY N. ABRAMS, INC., PUBLISHERS

Contents

Endpapers: The Summit Course at Cordillera, Edwards, Colorado. Hole 12, par-4.

Page 1: Desert Mountain, Cochise Course, Carefree, Arizona. Hole 13, par-3.

Pages 2 and 3: Bear's Club, Jupiter, Florida. Hole 7, par-3.

This page and opposite: Aspen Glen Golf Club, Carbondale, Colorado. Hole 15, par-4.

for CHARLIE

Foreword

From the time Jack Nicklaus was 10 years old, you'd hear his name in Ohio golf circles. But the first time I ever actually met him was in 1956. I was 30 years old and we were playing in an exhibition with Sam Snead at the Urbana (Ohio) Country Club. Jack was 16 years old and he was two-fisted that week, playing in both the Ohio Open at the Country Club in Marietta and the Snead exhibition. This kid played his first two rounds in Marietta (76 on Thursday, 70 on Friday morning), hopped on a private plane and flew to Urbana for the exhibition. He shot a 72 in the presence of Sam Snead, and then flew back to Marietta for the last two rounds. He finished 64–72 and won the Ohio Open. This was a special kid.

That marked the beginning of my lifelong wonderment at Jack the player, the person, and eventually the friend and golf course architect. Our lives have since intersected on various levels. We've had mutual friends throughout Ohio. We were both in the insurance business for a time, too. But, early on, we met most frequently

on the golf course. I'll never forget losing to Jack 3-and-2 in the hard-fought semifinal of the 1958 Trans-Mississippi Amateur. There I was, 32 years old, in my competitive prime, and 18-year-old Jackie Nicklaus was driving it at least 30 yards past me on every hole. My only solace was that after he beat me, he went on to become the youngest champion in the history of the event. We competed often. In fact, I'm proud to say I actually beat Jack by a few shots in the first two rounds of the 1957 U.S. Open at

Inverness, the first U.S. Open for which Jack ever qualified. The only problem was that neither of us went on to make the cut. Still, in my mind our most enjoyable and most enduring association came during our golf course design partnership. It wasn't particularly long or particularly prolific, but after competing against Jack and then having come to know him socially, I truly enjoyed my glimpse into his strategic and creative recesses.

Our design partnership came about in 1965, when Jack was 25 years old. I'd left the insurance business for golf course design, and was asked by a very successful Ohio businessman named Fred Jones to design The Golf Club in New Albany, Ohio. I was still very inexperienced as a golf course designer and this was an important project for me. It occurred to me one day that before I got too far along in the construction, I ought to have a player who knew something about golf come take a look. So I called Jack and asked if he would be willing to stop by and critique the course with me.

The first two holes went fine, but for some reason that I can't now explain, I had put in a round green surrounded by four round bunkers on the 185-yard par-3 3rd hole. I asked Jack what he thought, and without hesitating he said, "It looks bad." Then, after saying the words "boring" and "Mickey Mouse" in the same sentence, he reeled off an essay on how to improve the hole that would have made Donald Ross's jaw drop. He talked about tying this into that and moving this over there like he'd been designing for 20 years. It was as though all the things he'd learned about golf since his first days on the Scioto Golf Club practice tee with Jack Grout were now being recycled into coherent design strategy. Based on his critique, I went back and built a gigantic three-level bunker on the left-hand side of the green and used more than 450 railroad ties for bulkheading.

That critique led, a few years later, to our striking an informal association and eventually to our forming a partnership. We worked on four or five courses together, but the best-known fruit of that partnership is certainly Harbour Town Golf Links in Hilton Head, South Carolina. Since I was in my mid 40s when we took on that project and Jack was only 28, and since I was the design "veteran" of our twosome, most people assume I brought Jack in on that project. The fact is that Jack was the one who was originally approached for the job. He probably could have done it on his own, but he brought me in. He has always been gracious enough to give me the lion's share of the credit for Harbour Town, but the course would never have been so well accepted if it hadn't been for his involvement.

I'd like to say that I gave Jack his start in design back on the Golf Club job, but I think that designation really belongs to Bobby Jones. Other than his father, Charlie Nicklaus, I think Jones had the greatest impact on Jack in terms of personal deportment, golf course strategy, and golf course design. Jack is a second-shot thinker, as was Jones, meaning the crux of the game is not so much in the power of the tee ball as in the skill with which you play your approach to the green. While Jones really had a design hand in only two 18-hole courses—Augusta National and Peachtree Golf Club—that idea permeates both of them. I think Jack has consciously and unconsciously adhered to that philosophy throughout his career, and it has served him, his designs, and Jones's legacy very well.

Because I've worked with him so closely, people often ask me about Jack's place in the pantheon of golf course architects. Well, there have been golf course designers for centuries. But as of the early 1970s, when Jack got into the business, the idea of tying a course to an architect's name and that architect's particular style was unheard of. Ever wonder why so many Donald Ross courses no longer exist? It's because for a long time no one placed a value on a name. For the first 70 years that golf was played in the United States, a course was just a place to play golf, and the architect was no better known or regarded than the greenkeeper. Quick, how many greenkeepers can you name?

Jack changed all that. His mere presence in the business lent credibility to all of us. Established architects like Robert Trent Jones became even more successful. Only after Jack gave birth to the notion of tying a name to a course did veteran, retired, and even deceased designers begin to get the credit due them. Here's a good example. During World War II, I was stationed for a time at Fort Bragg, North Carolina. Through the good offices of a golf-loving colonel on base, I played Pinehurst No. 2 every day for six months. I loved golf and I was good at it. But back then, I honestly couldn't have told Donald Ross from Betsy Ross. Very few people could have. Today, you've got courses all over the world actively promoting themselves as Donald Ross designs. Jack was a huge part of that evolution in individual recognition. How appropriate that in 2001 Jack received the Donald Ross Award, the highest honor bestowed by the American Society of Golf Course Architects.

Jack's impact has been felt not only in the way golfers look at architects, but in the way golfers look at golf courses and in the way golf courses actually *look*. On his tournament courses, he was the first to focus not just on the course or the players, but also on the gallery. When I began work on the TPC at Sawgrass, which we were excitedly promoting as the "first stadium golf course," PGA Tour Commissioner Deane Beman quietly sent me to Ontario, Canada, to check out Jack's fan-friendly layout at Glen Abbey. He'd built it years earlier. Few people realize it, but it was there and at Muirfield Village that Jack actually built the first spectator mounds. People associate them with me and the TPC courses, but it was Jack who originated the idea of incorporating these mounds into the design of the golf course.

Jack also emphasized bunkering by making his bunkers more dramatic in appearance and more demanding in play. His golf courses jump out at you visually. And Jack was never afraid to incite a little controversy. When we were working on Harbour Town, Jack was giving me his thoughts on how we should do the 15th hole. When he completed his explanation, I said, "Sounds great, Jack, but that's gonna be hard as hell to play." He shrugged his shoulders. The design stands, and No. 15 is one of the best par-5s the PGA Tour plays every year.

As I said in my own book a few years ago, working with Jack on Harbour Town was a first-class experience. It's astonishing to me that the same guy who was gifted with the greatest golf skill of the 20th century should also be blessed with such deft creativity. Jack plays that down by saying that almost everything designers are doing today has already been done before, and that all we're doing now is reinterpreting existing ideas. If that's so, then one of the reasons Jack has been so successful is that he has a remarkable memory. Jack has undoubtedly played more golf courses all over the world than any architect in history. It's not an exaggeration to say that he remembers nearly everything about every one of them. With all those impressions filed away in his mind, he can retrieve them at will and tweak them as needed.

Our partnership lasted only a few years. Jack was thinking bigger than I was. He's been that way in everything he's ever done. I never really wanted to expand and Jack did. He threw himself into the design scene worldwide. I didn't. Those were lifestyle decisions made in mutual respect and understanding. I admire Jack. I have enormous regard for what he has accomplished and still is accomplishing in and for golf course design. I'm honored to have worked with him and to call him a friend, and I'm flattered that he asked me to contribute this foreword. I have no doubt that this beautiful book, which adorns your table today, will be devoured by students of golf course design for centuries to come. I just hope they learn as much from Jack as I did.

Pete Dye
2002
Indianapolis, Indiana

1 Breaking Ground

I'm not sure if golf course architects are born or if they're made. For me, I think it was a little of both.

I cannot count the number of times I played Scioto Country Club, my childhood course in Ohio, without even thinking about its design. All I thought about in those days was how to hit a ball farther, hit it better, or make par. Until I was in college, a high percentage of my golf was played at Scioto. I'd won a few junior tournaments in and around the Columbus area and a handful outside the state, but I didn't really have much to compare to my home course. In fact, my well-documented left-to-right style of play developed strictly because of Scioto, where about 11 out of 14 driving holes have either out-of-bounds right, serious trouble right, or at least encourage a left-to-right shot. I developed a left-to-right game simply because I had to if I was ever going to score well there.

Scioto obviously formed my thoughts for how to *play* golf, but I think it also helped formulate my earliest thoughts on how to design a golf course. Scioto is a Donald Ross design, and even though I've never really designed courses in the manner that Ross did, that particular course had a huge influence on my design career. The vehicle for that influence was none other than Bobby Jones. Jones won the 1926 U.S. Open at Ross's Scioto.

Throughout my childhood, I'd hear from my father and the older members where Jones drove it on this particular hole, or how he played that particular hole. Jones has had a huge personal influence on me, as a role model and, later in my career, as a friend. People ask me if that knowledge—the strategic template that Jones used to win the Open—has influenced my design philosophy, and the answer is both yes and no.

With Bobby Jones at the 1957 International Jaycee Jr. at the Ohio State University golf course in Columbus. Jones made a great impact on my career, not only as a competitor and role model, but through the design philosophy he and Alister Mackenzie employed at the Augusta National Golf Club.

In my early teens, I began
to travel and experience
new golf course designs.
In 1954, the year this pic-
ture was taken at the
Tri-State Championship,
I went to Los Angeles for
the U.S. Junior Cham-
pionship.

Overleaf: Muirfield Golf
Club, Lothian, Scotland.
This was the site of my
first overseas golf trip. It
had an enormous impact
on me as a young player
and as a future designer.

Jones influenced my design philosophy enormously, but not really through his competitive strategy at Scioto. It was more through his and Alister Mackenzie's *design* strategy
at Augusta National that he struck a nerve with me. Augusta's overarching philosophy is
to give you a lot of room off the tee, and then to place a premium on the second shot.
Most of my life I've played that way, what I call second-shot golf. The tee shot was
almost a formality for me. I'd step up to the tee, knock the ball out there, and then really
focus on the second shot to the green. Fortunately for me, that's the way Augusta has
been laid out for most of my career. So yes, Ross and Jones did enter into my thinking
on design. By winning at Ross's Scioto, Jones caught my attention. But it was Jones's
aura and his design philosophy, as limited as it was, that really influenced me.

In 1953, at the age of 13, I traveled to Tulsa, Oklahoma, to play in the United States
Golf Association (USGA) Junior Championship at Southern Hills. I still played primarily
in Ohio, but over the next few years I began to travel a little and see more courses, more
designs. I played in the U.S. Junior again in 1954, this time at Los Angeles Country
Club's North Course, designed by George C. Thomas, Jr. The next year, I played at
Purdue University's South Course in Lafayette, Indiana, designed by William H. Diddel.

Those three trips opened my eyes a little. In my teens, when I was making my first visit to a new course, I could just feel something that told me when a hole was special. If you play enough holes, you start to develop an eye for what works or doesn't work on a particular golf course or golf hole. It still wouldn't occur to me for years that I might be a golf course designer, but I was noticing more about design. I began to note differences from course to course in bunkering, green complexes, routing. I began to understand more clearly the signals that architects send, the strategy of a particular hole or course. But this was a lengthy process. At this time I was still very interested in other sports. Most people assume I was golf-focused as a kid, but I didn't really think about golf very seriously until late in high school. I may have paid attention to it in the summer, but come fall I was thinking football, in winter it was basketball, and in spring it was baseball and track.

My interest in golf really took hold for good in the spring of 1957, when I was 17 years old. The previous year I had played for the first time in a tournament staged primarily for professionals, the Ohio Open at Marietta Country Club. That was a magical few days. On Thursday and Friday, in the first and second rounds, I shot 76–70. But for Friday afternoon I had accepted a long-standing invitation to play with Sam Snead in an exhibition in Urbana. I flew to Urbana, met and played with Snead. From that point on, I began to devote myself more seriously to competitive golf. The fruit of that commitment was twofold: I improved as a player, and I was exposed to more and more varied golf course designs.

When I began to play in top-level international competitions such as the Walker Cup, the British Amateur, the U.S. Open, and the U.S. Amateur, my horizons expanded dramatically. I played on my first Walker Cup team in 1959. It was my first trip out of the United States. The venue was Muirfield, home of the Honourable Company of Edinburgh Golfers, the oldest golf club in the world. I fell in love with the place immediately. It showed me how varied golf courses can be. There was none of the meticulous grooming we associate with American golf courses, the ground was natural and rugged. History was everywhere.

Muirfield had a dramatic effect on me in many ways. I realized that I had some true potential as a player, and Muirfield opened my eyes to the history and the roots of the

game. My personal bond with Muirfield has been powerful. In 1966, seven years after my first wide-eyed visit, I returned to win the British Open. A few years later, I got involved in one of the most gratifying projects of my design career—a golf course development near my hometown of Columbus, Ohio. I tried to convey my affection and gratitude for the Scottish course by naming the project Muirfield Village and the club Muirfield Village Golf Club.

My introduction to Scottish golf and international competition came in 1959, but I also played in a handful of PGA Tour events that year as an amateur. Being out there on a more frequent basis with the world's top professional players forced me to hone my game, and it opened my eyes a little more to the strategic side of golf. On tougher golf courses, with tougher competition, I had to think more specifically about my angle into the green: What type of shot would leave the easiest putt? Where was the best place to miss the green? When should I blast away off the tee and when should I rein it in? When to charge a putt and when to lag? The only way I could really answer those questions was to analyze the golf course. In trying to refine my strategy, I became more engrossed in design. It was not just interest, it was necessary that I better manage my game if I was to become a better player. After that, it was not a very big leap from "How should I play this hole?" to "Why did he design it this way?"

I think youngsters tend to get caught up in the competition, that is, beating other players or hitting a ball longer than their friends can. When you really start looking at golf holes and particular golf shots from a strategic standpoint, the true beauty of the game presents itself. That's when you learn that golf is really about playing the course, about beating the golf course rather than the other players.

It wasn't until the early 1960s that I dipped my toe into golf course design. By then, Scioto had become a little ragged around the edges, and the club hired Dick Wilson to rejuvenate the course. I made a habit of tagging along on Dick's site visits. He was an accomplished golf course designer, but I never really understood what he did at Scioto. He did not restore the course—he redesigned it. He delegated the front nine restoration to Robert von Hagge, who was working for him at the time. The back nine went to another associate, Joe Lee. The result was that they turned what had been a great 18-hole golf course into two distinctly different 9-hole courses. It was still a nice golf

The opening round at Muirfield Village Golf Club, 1974. I played with Tom Weiskopf (walking in front), Johnny Miller (with me), and Lee Trevino (not in the photo).

course, but not the Ross course I had grown up on. Although I had no design hand in this renovation, I did learn a lesson from the final product. A golf course needs a sense of continuity. I've designed a lot of golf courses in which the front and back run through different terrain, but in those cases I've tried to make sure that the strategy, style, options, and shot values for both nines remain similar.

Five years after that, I waded a little deeper into golf course design after a phone call from an Indiana insurance man turned golf course designer. His name was Pete Dye. I had known Pete for some time. During my amateur career, I was also in the insurance business. He was from Urbana, Ohio, I was from Columbus, and we'd played amateur golf together quite a few times. He was a very good player and had won the Indiana Amateur in 1958 after finishing second twice. In 1959, Pete ditched a very successful insurance career and replaced it with his true love, golf course design.

One of Pete's first projects was The Golf Club in New Albany, Ohio. Fred Jones, who owned the Ohio State Life Insurance Co., was behind the project (coincidentally, while an amateur a few years earlier, I had also worked for OSLI). Pete just called me one day and asked me to come out and see his work, so I did. Pete tells the story of that day in the Foreword to this book. In spite of his more than generous appraisal of my role, I really didn't have a whole lot of input, but he thought I could help him and I tried.

He called me not long afterwards and said, "How about doing some consulting with me on some golf courses? I think we'd have a lot of fun together." I said sure. Those were my baby steps into the business. I wouldn't even have presumed to think of myself as a golf course architect at that point (in fact, I've always struggled with describing myself as an architect, because the term suggests a certain level of organized education. I've always preferred "golf course designer." Anyone can design, but to me, only graduates of a designated program are architects). I felt more like a summer intern.

Then Mark McCormack, the agent who was overseeing my business interests at that time, said he'd been contacted by Standard Oil of California, that they wanted to build a golf course in the Long Beach oil fields and wanted me to consult, along with Press Maxwell. I didn't know it at the time, but later learned that Press was the son of golf course designer Perry Maxwell (who created Southern Hills in Tulsa among other

courses), and that the son was an accomplished designer in his own right.

Well, I was young and excited and flew out there, got myself to the property, walked it with Press, and asked him what my role, my involvement, would be. I'll never forget his answer.

"None," he said bluntly.

I said, "Well, what about my suggestions, are you going to use anything?"

"May not use anything," he replied. "Probably won't."

I called Standard Oil, gave them their money back on the spot, and that was it. They ended up building a golf course there, but I don't know anything about it. I take some pride in the fact that at 28 years old I was able to walk away from a situation that presented plenty of money but no credibility. It sounds obvious, but you've got to be paid to do a job and you've got to do something to be paid. Otherwise, there's no credibility in the person or the project. I would have been in the position of collecting my fee ($25,000 for the Standard Oil job) when I knew that Maxwell had no intention of using anything I did. I would have diluted my reputation in design before my career even got started.

Not long after that Mark called with another offer. This one was for real. A developer named Charles Fraser had asked him about my designing a golf course for him on Hilton Head Island in South Carolina. I checked with Pete to see if he wanted in on the project. He came on board, and that was the real start to my career in the design business.

The golf course, Harbour Town Golf Links, was very well received, and it appeared as though I was on my way. But, looking back on that project, I can see what a novice I was. I may have had some instincts for design, but I had very few instincts for managing a business. I made 23 trips to that golf course at various points during the design and construction, and never got any of my expenses out of it. I think our design fee was $40,000, all of which Pete put right back into the golf course. That's the way it was, though. Ever the artist, Pete wasn't in it for the money as much as for the love of doing design. That approach was fine for me too. I would have liked the money, but I didn't care about the fee as much as I did about the valuable experience. A few years ago, Pete and I both spoke at an American Society of Golf Course Architects banquet and I remember ribbing him in front of the crowd that I lost money on Harbour Town. When Pete got to the podium he said, "Yeah, that's all you were worth."

Whereas I was marginally involved in the final outcome of The Golf Club, Harbour Town was the first time I had a hand in almost every hole. Still, I was hardly what you would call a designer. I was just getting my feet wet, but I enjoyed it.

After Harbour Town, I did a few more courses with Pete. Each one was an adventure. We did a fun little course in Lake Geneva, Wisconsin, called Dogpatch, and two courses at Johns Island. Our last one was Wabeek Golf Club in Bloomfield Hills, Michigan.

As I said earlier, Pete is the consummate artist and I respect that. He is the best. He loves and is superbly talented at developing both a strategic and aesthetic vision for a golf course. Working with Pete was tremendous fun, very informative, and a great learning experience, but I began to want to express myself more freely and be more on my own. It was then that Pete and I amicably dissolved our partnership. There wasn't any rancor. It was the right thing to do. Pete is enormously talented and really didn't need me anyway. We've stayed good friends ever since, and I was delighted that he agreed to write the Foreword to this book.

Even though my apprenticeship in golf course design was not complete, I had pretty much made up my mind that I was going to design and build a course in or near my hometown of Columbus, Ohio. In fact, as far back as 1966, I began buying up land in nearby Dublin just for this purpose. What few people know is that I actually had Pete work up a couple of early routings for the land. But once we parted, I began to look around for someone else, another partner who had development experience and a land-planning background as well as golf course design experience. I found a man named Put Pierman, who put the finances for Muirfield Village together and also began working with me on my business affairs. Put came up with a designer named Desmond Muirhead. Desmond had the eclectic background I'd been looking for. Born in Great

Harbour Town Golf Links, hole 3, par-4.

Overleaf, pages 24 and 25: Harbour Town Golf Links, Hilton Head Island, South Carolina. Hole 18, par-4. Harbour Town opened in 1970. It's really a Pete Dye design, I was just a consultant. But it was the first course on which I had design input on almost every hole.

Overleaf, pages 26 and 27: Harbour Town Golf Links, Hilton Head Island, South Carolina. Hole 7, par-3. The experience I gained here was priceless.

Britain, he'd studied both architecture and engineering at Cambridge University. Beyond that, he'd studied horticulture in Canada and the United States.

Desmond was an iconoclast. In the early 1960s, before he'd really begun designing courses, he'd made a tour of the great golf courses of the United Kingdom and North America. After his survey, which included some of the most highly regarded courses in Scotland and the United States, he said, "These courses have no mystique whatsoever. I owe very little allegiance to St. Andrews." Not exactly my sentiments, but at least my new partner wouldn't be shy about expressing his opinions. Where my previous partner, Pete, was a pure designer, Desmond and his land-planning background brought the ability not only to help design a golf course, but to integrate the course with the surrounding real estate and shape the two of them together.

I continued to accumulate land in Dublin, and Desmond and I continued to "doodle" plans for it, but in the meantime we worked on several other projects together. We did two golf courses at King's Island, outside Cincinnati—the Bruin Course and the Grizzly Course. Those were public course projects, and since I had had very little experience in public courses up to that point, Desmond took the lead there. Then we did New St. Andrews in Japan, followed by Mayacoo Lakes in West Palm Beach, Florida, and La Moraleja in Madrid.

By 1974, we had completed Muirfield Village and I was again feeling the need to spread my wings. I didn't have any particular falling-out with Desmond, but increasingly I wanted to do my own thing. Getting input from someone else too often made me feel that in order to honor the partnership I had to compromise my vision for the golf course. Eventually, I decided that if I was ever really going to pursue golf course design in a serious way, I'd probably have to do it myself. So Desmond and I parted ways. He went off to finish the Kings Island courses and I finished up La Moraleja, Mayacoo Lakes and, of course, my pet project back in Columbus.

By the mid 1970s, after hands-on tutorials with Pete Dye and Desmond Muirhead in which I worked on a total of nine golf courses, I felt as though I had enough fundamental experience to go out on my own. Harbour Town was a success. Muirfield Village had been open for a couple of years and was getting some solid reviews. But although these particular golf courses were very well received, the overall critiques of my early solo projects were mixed. Some said they were too tough. Others said they were too bland. But almost all the critics of my early work had one complaint in common: Nicklaus designed golf courses that only Nicklaus could play, i.e., they were long and/or they favored a fade. To some extent the critics were right. As I mentioned earlier, my impressions of how a golf course should be played and, prior to that, how a course should be designed, were formed very early. Long and left-to-right had been second nature to me since my early days at Scioto. After I designed my first few golf courses, people started saying, "Nicklaus must have designed this golf course, because it plays left to right." In truth, I designed the way I played. I visualize all my shots before I play them, and I did the same thing with my golf holes, visualizing each hole and each shot as though I was the one who was going to play it. The fact that the vast majority of amateurs slice the ball didn't help much. If there was trouble on the right they found it quickly, and it seemed like I heard about it soon thereafter.

I can be as stubborn as the next guy, but eventually I began to listen to the critics. I started trying to balance my work. This was a significant step for me as a designer and for the quality of my designs. I began to insert as much left-right/right-left balance as I could, and that led to a broader appreciation of balance in all aspects of a golf course design. After mixing left with right, I soon realized that a short par-3 should be balanced with a long par-3, short par-5s need to be accompanied by long par-5s, and a couple of long par-4s need to be mixed in with a couple of short ones and a few medium-length holes.

The learning curve that began back in high school was continuing (and still is). I've played, by my best count, approximately 500 golf courses. They say that every person you meet has some influence on you, even if you're not aware of it. I think the same can be said for golf courses. Each of them has had some impact on my thinking. It may not always be on a conscious level, but the impact is there.

Over the years I've actually picked up more pointers on what *not* to do than what to

Overleaf: Harbour Town Golf Links, Hilton Head Island, South Carolina. Hole 9, par-4.

do. You pick up things to do because you find a hole you like. You may like the way it fits into the terrain or the way it plays from slope to counterslope (a concept we'll delve into later on). You might like the way the fairway or the green accepts the golf ball. But even with a good hole, if you pick it apart you can usually find something you don't like about it. For instance, I've seen terrific long par-4s where everything's done just beautifully but the green is too small to accept the long-iron second shots that the architect has demanded. So, over time, the learning process for me has been to retain the good things and build on them while making note of the bad ones and trying not to repeat them.

That's how I work. I take holes I like and ideas I like, and then I try to apply them to my golf courses. All the while I try not to make mistakes in terms of fairness, severity, proportions, aesthetics, and balance.

Muirfield Village Golf Club, Dublin, Ohio. Hole 8, par-3.

2 Philosophy

I don't have a strict philosophy of golf course design. I think they can be very limiting. There are a handful of constants, however, that go into my approach on just about every project I do. Basically, I look at any project we consider from four angles:

Who is going to play the course?

How sensitive is the environment?

How can I balance the demands on a player's intelligence with demands on his strength?

How will it look? It sounds basic, but a golf course has to be pretty.

1. Who is going to play the course?

It doesn't matter if you're in the insurance business or the movie business or the business of designing golf courses. In the end, the customer determines everything. Your competition can say what they want about your product, but ultimately the customer decides whether your product has a market. So it only makes sense that the customer—the man, woman, or child who's going to be using your product—be a big part of your thinking from day one.

Muirfield Village Golf Club, Dublin, Ohio. Hole 5, par-5. From its inception, this course was designed with a PGA Tour event in mind—to provide a championship test to skilled players. Hole 5, pictured here, measures approximately 527 yards.

That sounds obvious, but you'd be amazed at how often developers and designers (including myself in my early days) are completely oblivious to it. My customer is either going to be the varied membership of a private club, the even more varied public course player who ponies up his daily fee, a vacation-minded guest at a resort hotel, possibly a tour professional, or all/some of the above combined.

Then I need to know what my client, the developer, wants. Is he looking for a player-friendly course or for a serious championship test? Is he looking for something even more serious? Does he have hopes of hosting a significant amateur or professional tournament someday? These issues are critical not only from the standpoint of course difficulty, but from a maintenance angle as well. Some of the more challenging elements of tournament courses—sloping greens, contoured fairways, deep rough—are more costly to create and maintain than the basic features found on most courses.

"Who is going to play the course?" It's such a simple thing, but I learned about it the hard way. As we've discussed, my courses were often tagged "too hard" or "made for Nicklaus." And my early courses certainly were made for tournament play. Take a look at some of my early collaborations and solo designs:

MUIRFIELD VILLAGE was designed for a developer (my own group) who wanted a seriously challenging golf course that would, we hoped, host a serious tournament. As it turned out, Muirfield has hosted the Memorial Tournament since the event's inception in 1976, and has also hosted the Ryder Cup, the U.S. Amateur, the U.S. Junior, the Solheim Cup, and the Wendy's 3-Tour Challenge.

THE GREENBRIER COURSE was originally built in 1924 by Seth Raynor and George O'Neil. In 1977, I was brought in specifically to redesign the course for the 1979 Ryder Cup. It is the only resort golf course in the world to have been the host site for both the Ryder Cup Matches and the Solheim Cup Matches (1994).

GLEN ABBEY was my first solo design. My client, the Royal Canadian Golf Association, wanted to build a permanent home for Canada's most prestigious event. In addition to hosting 23 Canadian Opens, it has hosted the DuMaurier Classic, which until 2000 was a major championship on the LPGA Tour.

The Greenbrier Course, White Sulphur Springs, West Virginia. Hole 2, par-4. My work on this course was done with world-class professional play in mind.

*Glen Abbey Golf
Club, Oakville, Ontario.
Hole 12, par-3. Glen
Abbey was designed to
host the Canadian Open
Championship.*

*Overleaf: Shoal Creek
Golf Club, Birmingham,
Alabama. Hole 17, par-5.
In its relatively brief life,
Shoal Creek has hosted
two PGA Championships
(1984, 1990) and a U.S.
Amateur Championship
(1986).*

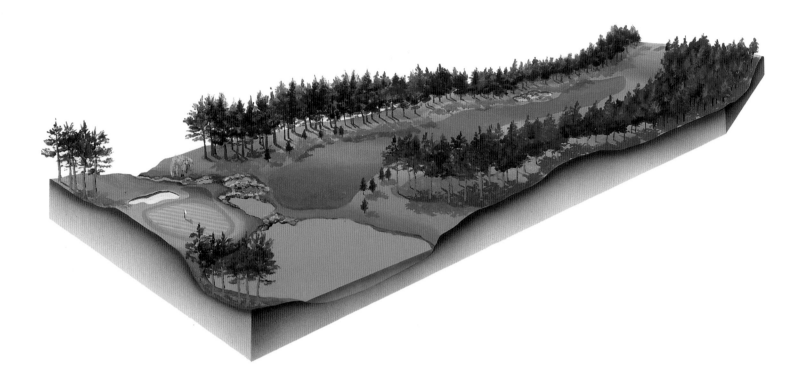

Shoal Creek Golf Club, hole 17, par-5. Birmingham, Alabama.

SHOAL CREEK has hosted two PGA Championships and a U.S. Amateur.

THE AUSTRALIAN GOLF CLUB has hosted several Australian Opens.

These early courses were difficult, but they were supposed to be, and they attracted some of the most prestigious titles and some of the best fields in the game. However, several of my early job assignments should have been to design a golf course that could not only host a golf tournament with a world-class field, but one that could *also* accommodate the desires and the skill levels of amateur golfers. Over time, with the help of experience and the odd critic, I've learned to balance those seemingly contradictory elements.

   The best example of that is right in my own backyard. I've probably spent more time at Muirfield Village putting in changes for the membership than I have putting in changes for the Memorial Tournament. For example, there's No. 6. It had a big tree

short and right of the green. And as that tree grew, the members just could not play the hole. Members never want change; they loved that tree, but we took it out and put fairway in the front right. It doesn't affect the tournament player at all, but it definitely affects the member playing into that green. Then I added some green in the back left to make a more difficult pin placement for the tournament.

We enlarged the 8th, 9th, and 12th greens for the membership, and we created bounce-ins on No. 11 and 16 for them. We opened 15 up a little bit—lowered the green and made it a little easier for the member to get into. When the green was higher, most members were close in and playing their third shot from a low area. When the green was higher, they couldn't see any of the pin. Now that the green is a little lower, they get a much better idea of where the pin is. We changed tee placements with the members in mind on some holes, and widened some fairways in the shorter areas off the tee.

Australian Club, Kensington, Australia.

Overleaf: Muirfield Village Golf Club, Dublin, Ohio. Hole 12, par-3.

Kings Island in Mason, Ohio, is an object lesson in the importance of knowing who is going to play your course. When I began work there with Desmond, it was to be strictly for public play, no thought of a tournament or anything else. Since I was then focusing more on tournament courses and private clubs, I pretty much let Desmond handle the project. It was fine for the average recreational player, but there was nothing to challenge a tour player— because there weren't going to be any tour events.

Then, all of a sudden, the owners decided they wanted to host the Ohio Kings Island Open, a PGA Tour event. For years from that point on, every time I went back to Mason I spent time trying to change the course from a mild-mannered public facility into a challenging test of tournament golf. We must have done something right because today, almost 30 years and I don't know how many hours of surgery later, they're still playing a Senior PGA Tour event there.

Had I known at the start that they wanted to host a tour event, I would have designed a tournament course and tweaked it to accommodate public play. That's much more practical than trying to do the reverse.

As important as the question "*Who* is going to play the course?" is the question "*How* are they going to play the course?" And by that I mean we now have to take modern equipment, particularly the ball, into account when we design golf courses. That's fairly easy to do. What's difficult is adapting or redesigning our great old courses to keep them competitive. More on this later.

Muirfield Village Golf Club, Dublin, Ohio. Hole 15, par-5. At this 503-yard hole, we took pains to open up the green and give all players—professional and amateur—a better view of their target. We also made it more challenging for the pro who wishes to reach the green in two shots.

2. How sensitive is the environment?

There may be no better marriage between development and environment than a golf course. In fact, contrary to the belief of many environmental activists, the best golf courses very often have the least impact on the land. Why? The answer goes all the way back to the roots of golf course design. A golf course should fit the terrain it's being built on. Look at the original Muirfield or St. Andrews in Scotland. There's nothing artificial or synthetic about either of them. Look at just about any of the golf courses in the British Open rota. They flow with the landscape.

I take my design cues from nature. I try never to force an idea onto a piece of land, and I think most of the top designers today would agree that a big part of our job is not so much disrupting earth, but taking the suggestions of Mother Nature and building on them. We let the surroundings shape the holes we create.

While that happens to be the way I work, it also meshes well with the current political climate. Environmental rules are extremely strict in the United States and getting stricter all the time. Indeed, I probably could not have built Muirfield Village today. The 2nd, 3rd , 5th, 6th, 9th, 11th, 12th, 14th , and 18th holes are all built on flood plains. We could build golf holes there today, but they'd have to take a drastically different form. The creeks probably couldn't be touched, so the course and the individual holes couldn't have relationships to them. It's a good example of how the rules have changed in the design business. And while you might expect someone who makes a living designing golf courses to object to that, I actually welcome the restrictions. I love nature. I enjoy being part of an undisturbed natural setting. The desire to be outdoors and in nature is one of the things that drew me to golf as a kid and still does today. I'm lucky that my design associates do most of the preliminary negotiating with the various government commissions and environmental agencies, but I do make the design decisions on how to work within those agencies' final guidelines.

To use a recent example, one of my most recent courses, The Bear's Club, is about a mile from the Atlantic Ocean in Jupiter, Florida. We had to stay an average of 25 feet from all wetlands throughout the golf course and cover the area in between with a gradual slope and wetlands or upland plants. We were allowed to get within 15 feet in some areas as long as we compromised in others. I have no problem at all with that, particularly when the rules are clear and reasonable. One very positive difference between now and 15 years ago is that today we are getting clearer decisions based on clearer rules. Fifteen years ago, when environmentalism first impacted the golf course design business, no one really knew what the rules were. Every federal, state, and local agency had its own definitions of things, or made things up as they went along. They couldn't even interpret basic questions such as what comprised a wetland. You'd ask them, "Can we do this here?" and they'd say "No." Then we'd say, "Well, what can we do?" And they'd say, "You can't do anything." In certain places you still get that a lot. I really don't mind a "no," but at least tell me what I *can* do.

The rules are now generally clear for the most part, and the various agencies are increasingly on the same page. Once we have the information from environmental agencies, the fun begins. Golf course design is very much a puzzle to begin with. Once you have some restrictions placed on you, it forces you to be even more creative in solving the puzzle.

The United States has the toughest restrictions on land development of any country I can think of. Many people don't realize this, but it's a lot easier to build a golf course or develop land overseas. I'm proud of the fact that even when we work in countries with less restrictive rules, we voluntarily apply United States rules to all Nicklaus Design work. For instance, at the Four Seasons Punta Mita in Mexico we built a stunning island par-3 out in the Pacific Ocean. We got it done because of the way we approached the project environmentally. To water the hole, we laid pipes that let us hydrate, drain, and fertilize the grass internally. Nothing was going to contaminate the area. I'm not sure we had to do all that under Mexico's environmental rules, but I'm glad we did—the island green there may be the prettiest coastal green in the world.

I can't think of any project we've done in recent years where wildlife hasn't increased significantly from what it was when we began. At Muirfield Village, we have a 17-acre area in the middle of the golf course where there are three houses. On that parcel today we have a larger deer population than we did when we built the golf course. They come out and feed around the course itself and nest inside the woods. We have tremendous bird life around the course. Even with the lack of rules in the 1970s, we didn't damage the population at all. We're not about to do it now.

Overleaf: Mount Juliet, County Kilkenny, Ireland. Hole 3, par-3. The River Noir runs through this former horse farm. In sensitive overseas environments such as this one, we voluntarily apply strict U.S. environmental rules.

Above: Silt fences like this one are used to keep silt out of pristine areas. Thousands of feet of this material are used to protect a sensitive environment.

Left: This gopher tortoise was found on site during construction of The Bear's Club. We take pains to protect wildlife at all our sites.

Opposite: The Bear's Club, Jupiter, Florida. Hole 2, par-3. In fragile environments such as the site for this course, strict guidelines protect the surroundings. I actually welcome such restrictions, for besides protecting the land they add another element to the puzzle that makes golf course design so interesting.

Overleaf: Four Seasons Golf Club, Punta Mita, Mexico. Hole 3B, par-3. Hydration, drainage, and fertilization for this stunning island par-3 are completely self-contained.

Ducks on a pond at the Muirfield Village Golf Club, Dublin, Ohio.

Opposite: The Golf Club of Purchase, Purchase, New York. Hole 10, par-4. Environmental regulations sometimes affect the final design. For example, the fairways at the Golf Club of Purchase are very narrow primarily because we had so little land with which to work.

The Golf Club of Purchase, just outside New York City, is a beautiful combination of uplands and wetlands, and the authorities were extremely aggressive in preserving the environment. Because they were so strict, we had very little land to work with, so most of the fairways are extremely narrow. In fact, they are so narrow and the surrounding trees so tall and numerous that I had some concerns about how well we'd be able to grow grass, but they've done a beautiful job. It's a magnificent golf course. Purchase is a perfect example of how thoughtful golf course design and preservation can coexist.

We were actually called in to rehabilitate an area on a couple of projects. Prior to being turned into a golf course, the TPC of Michigan site was literally and figuratively a dump. We found old automobiles, trash of every kind, toxic waste, oil—anything you want to think of was there. *Anything* we did to that property would have been an improvement. There wasn't a decent tree on the whole site. We're talking about a vast wasteland. Eleven years later, it's a model of restoration. In 1996, Audubon International presented us with its special recognition award for course design work that "exemplifies the finest in ecological reconstruction." I'm extremely proud of our work there.

Old Works Golf Club in Anaconda, Montana, is one of the most interesting projects I've ever worked on. There was a rich local history dating back more than a hundred years. The area had suffered economically, and the environmental situation was incredibly complex. We were able to salvage some local history, help the economy, improve the environment, and produce a terrific golf course.

Montana was one of the leading producers of copper at the turn of the century, and Anaconda was a boomtown built on mining and smelting. It prospered until the early 1900s, when the Anaconda Works was surpassed by the nearby Washoe smelter. Anaconda became a near ghost town. The copper-smelting facility upon which we

The TPC of Michigan, Dearborn. Hole 12, par-3. The site on which we designed the TPC of Michigan was one of the worst I have ever seen. You name it, we found it on that site—including old cars, tires, and, if I am not mistaken, even the proverbial kitchen sink. When the course opened in 1990, the site was unrecognizable. In place of the wasteland with which we had begun, there was now a virtual wildlife sanctuary. In fact, Audubon International honored the course in 1996 for its "ecological reconstruction."

would build a golf course was idle until 1983, and during those 80-or-so years, the land
grew impossibly contaminated by the remnants of the copper-mining era. In the mid
1980s it was designated a federal Superfund clean-up site. Despite the fact that no
Superfund site had ever been rehabilitated into useful land, Anaconda's citizens, along
with Arco, which now owned the land, formed a group to promote the construction of
a world-class golf course on the site. They deserve a lot of credit. They took something
that a lot of people said couldn't be done and they got it done.

The Environmental Protection Agency was all over the project, and rightfully so.
We broke ground in May of 1994 and had two EPA inspectors on the golf course
throughout the nearly two years of construction. We had to line massive portions of the
property to make sure that the residue from the defunct smelting operations didn't contaminate any nearby streams through runoff. We do that anyway during construction of
a golf course, but at Old Works the barriers between the golf course and the world are
permanent. They're underground. We'd take an entire green and line it underneath,
almost like slipping it into a plastic bag, to keep any fertilizers or chemicals from leach-
ing out.

Now, most places are careful about runoff of chemicals used on golf courses. If your
drainage is well designed, those waste products usually drain well away from streams.
They simply flow into the ground, dissipating away. But the primary guideline at
Old Works was that *nothing*, not the dirt from construction, not their superintendent's
fertilizer, and certainly not the residue from the old mine's chemicals was to get through.
Ever. We had to insulate all the streams. We had to clean up everything that
was there.

One of the most interesting aspects of that golf course is that we incorporated the
black slag that had been left over from the years of smelting. There were mountains of
the stuff, and we didn't really know what to do with it. Once the lab was able to
show us that it was inert and harmless, we decided to put it to work. We used it as
landforms for mounding, we used it as background and laid green patches through it,
we built tee boxes on it. Just out of curiosity, we had it tested for play as bunker sand,
too. To my amazement, it performed beautifully, so we put it in the bunkers. It was a
safe, visually stunning way to include the proud history of Anaconda in the golf course.

The severe environmental problems presented by Old Works made it one of the most expensive golf courses ever built. Had Old Works been built on a similar piece of land, but without all the contamination and subsequent EPA oversight, it would have been a $5 to $6 million project. The intense oversight from the government and from the owner, the Arco Corporation, put the final tab at about $23 million. That sounds like a lot of money, but I've been told that if they had done the project only as a restoration—no golf course, just land rehabilitation—it would have cost Arco $45 million. So even though it was a ridiculously expensive product, it's been a huge win for Arco, which saved over $20 million. It was a huge win for environmental science in that it was the first time that a federal Superfund site had ever successfully been given a second chance. It was a win for me and my design staff because we learned some extraordinary lessons about rehabilitating troubled land, chief among them the fact that it can be done. Most important, it's been a boon for the people of Anaconda and the surrounding area. The course brought jobs and quality, affordable public golf to an area that had seen some pretty hard times.

A few years after the course opened, I was chatting with some of the EPA guys who were with us on the project. One said, "Jack, we've gone through this now and we've succeeded. One thing we learned is that if we ever do it again, we probably don't have to be so tough. We did what we were required to do, but reasonableness tells us that we probably went too far." That was a good lesson for both of us.

Testing the bunker sand at Old Works Golf Club, Anaconda, Montana. The land was not the only thing we recycled at Old Works. We found surprising new uses for the black slag that had littered the property for decades.

Overleaf: Old Works Golf Club, Anaconda, Montana. Hole 14, par-4. This hole combines all the elements that make Anaconda such an interesting place. In addition to its beautiful surroundings and slag bunkers, its name, "Carroll Town," refers to a nearby company town that was painted entirely in red.

Old Works Golf Club,
Anaconda, Montana.
Hole 5, par-4.

3. Intelligence vs Strength

Golf has undergone a real evolution in the last 20 years. The combination of modern golf clubs, golf balls (which in my opinion simply go too far), and highly skilled athletes entering the game has put added pressure on golf course architects. We're now forced to find ways to test the increasingly long long-hitters without leaving the average or lesser player behind.

The fact is that you can never negate the advantage of length—assuming, of course, that the long-hitter is also hitting it fairly straight. But what you *can* do as a golf course architect is create enough variety so that over the course of 18 holes the player who can position the ball can compete with the person who powers the ball. That way, it's intelligence *and* strength that determine success. I see golf as a thinking person's game, both as a competitor and as a golf course designer. There's little challenge in just whacking a golf ball. A course has to offer variety for every golfer, no matter his or her level of skill or degree of strength. Many people actually assume my golf courses are all long monsters because I was generally regarded as a long hitter, a power player. Actually, I

see the emphasis on length as the worst fault in golf course design today. An architect
should require both power and intelligence, just as a player should employ both.

Take the 14th hole at Muirfield Village. You can go ahead and drive the ball over the
creek if you want to, if you have the power. It's a big advantage, and every once in
while we get some guys who do it. They knock it over the left side of the creek, and
even if they put it in the rough, they just have a little chip up there to the green. The
flip side is that you face a pretty difficult shot if you try to power it over the left side of
the creek and miss. How does the less powerful but more strategic player compete with
that? Easy. If he can position the ball off the tee, he'll end up with a very playable shot
into the green himself.

To me, there are a couple of elements at work in the Intelligence vs Strength debate.
Let's not forget that there are players out there who possess both attributes. On truly
great golf holes, they are eventually forced to make a decision between the two. To me,
a great golf hole provides all three players—the power player, the thinker, and the guy
who's got both—with options, and forces him to make one or more decisions.

The Bear's Club, Jupiter, Florida. Hole 5, par-4. This hole demands two different strategies, depending on pin position.

Take the 5th at the Bear's Club, a par-4 that plays 354 yards from the back tee. If the pin is in the front of the green, I'll take a driver so I can play left and close to the water to allow me to have the easiest angle into the green and not have to play to the narrow part of the green. But if the pin is in the middle or the back of the green, I'll play a little less club off the tee—no need to challenge the water on the tee shot, because the second shot into the green is not as demanding, but will be considerably longer. It is a tradeoff—challenge the tee shot and leave an easier second, or back off on the tee and leave a more demanding second shot.

Par-5s are always going to be the power man's game, and I don't think architects should try to take that away from him. You might make him play a dangerous shot, but as long as he can deliver, I say don't take choice out of the equation. That's why I like to include an "unreachable" par-5 in my designs, one that very few players can reach. An example of these marathon par-5s is the 10th hole at Colleton River in Bluffton, South Carolina. Very few people can reach that green in two.

In addition to a long 5, I'll usually have one that just about everybody can reach under normal conditions. A perfect example of the reachable par-5 is the 13th hole at Augusta National. It's only 465 yards long, but the problems that await you almost every foot of the way—Rae's Creek, the trees, the creek again, the slope of the fairway and the green itself—make it one of the great reachable par-5s in the world. I understand they've made some changes now to lengthen it by moving the tee back about 30 yards. I don't think it affects the strategy very much, but in its original form it was a beauty.

Then there are the long par-4s. Here the long hitter is going to have an advantage, and I think he should, as long he can keep it in play. Think about the 9th hole at Pebble Beach. A lot of times you get the wind blowing right in your face. A long hitter has a tremendous advantage because he can drive the ball over the hill and get some excess roll. As a result, he'll probably be left with a middle or short iron into the green. The shorter hitter is stuck back on top of the hill, hitting a long iron or a wood into a flattish green that doesn't want to accept a low trajectory shot. The long hitter clearly has an edge there. Conversely, on short par-4s the longer hitter may be forced to throttle back and the more placement-oriented guy can get an advantage by playing the right shot.

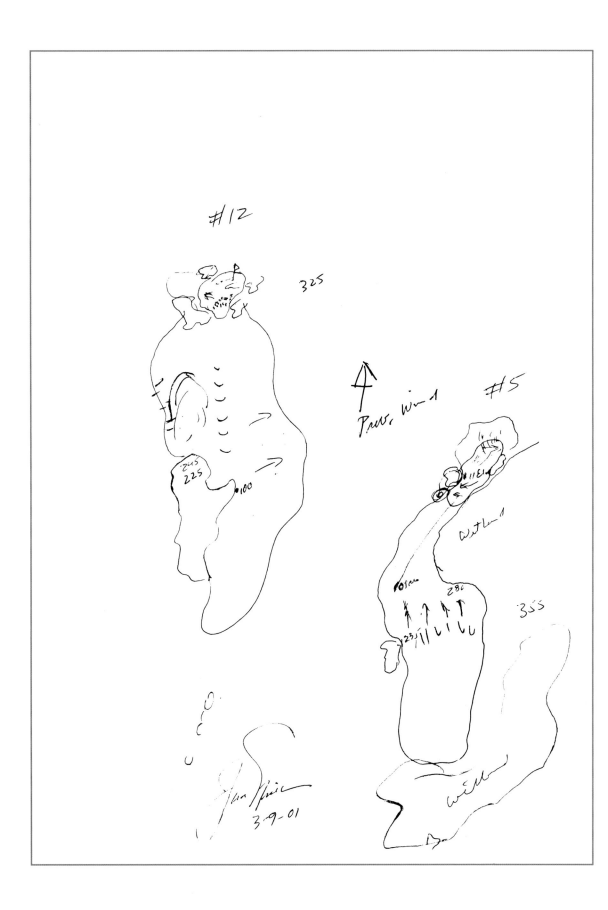

#12

325

Prev. Wind

#5

225
225

100

Wetland

286

235

355

Willow

3-9-01

My sketches of holes 12 and 5 at *The Bear's Club, Jupiter, Florida*. Both are strategic gems.

Overleaf: Colleton River Plantation, Bluffton, South Carolina. Hole 10, par-5. I like to have at least one "unreachable" par-5 in each of my golf course designs. While that does not mean it has never been reached in two, at 612 yards the 10th at Colleton River is relatively safe. The hole is nicknamed "Baltusrol" after the devilish 17th hole on the legendary U.S. Open course.

All illustrations on these pages: Augusta National Golf Club, Augusta, Georgia. Hole 13, par-5. If you are looking for a great, reachable par-5, it is pretty hard to beat the 13th at Augusta. As you can see in the photo above and the illustration to the left, Jones and Mackenzie did a terrific job of bringing the natural elements to bear in one of the ultimate risk-reward holes in golf.

*Visiting the site of my
hole 5 redesign at Pebble
Beach Golf Links, Pebble
Beach, California*

*Opposite: Pebble Beach
hole 9, par-4. At about
450 yards, and often into
the wind, this hole, like
most par-4s, gives the
big hitter a tremendous
advantage.*

I like to have at least one short par-3, because it's always fun to play that short, delicate hole, but I like to make sure that if you miss the green you've got some real work to
do to get up and down. To me, a great example of the short 3 is the "postage stamp
green" at Royal Troon in Scotland. It's just a little 8- or 9-iron shot. Sounds easy, right?
But you hit a little to the right, and you're dead as a doornail. You try to protect it to
the left, and you've got a nearly impossible up-and-down.

One of the really overlooked battlegrounds in the war between power and placement
is the driveable par-4. Some players call them gimmicky. I happen to enjoy them,
because it's all about decisions. The driveable par-4 offers a better-than-average reward
(eagle) for a better-than-average shot. I've always felt as though a good driveable par-4
can really reveal a player. The 10th hole at Riviera has always been a favorite of mine,
and the 12th hole at The Bear's Club is a really neat example. It's about 335 yards from
the back tee, and the prevailing wind is at the golfer's back. The bunker on the left side
of the fairway is about a 240-yard carry. It's a slight dogleg left and features a crowned

76

Royal Troon Golf Club, Troon, Scotland. Hole 8, par-3. This hole's world-famous "Postage Stamp" green makes it a very challenging par-3.

*Earlier sketches of the
12th hole at The Bear's
Club, Jupiter, Florida.
Hole 12 is a really neat,
driveable par-4. Pin placement and wind can height-
en the risk-reward factor,
but they can also give the
shorter player a big assist,
depending on the day.
(See also page 71).*

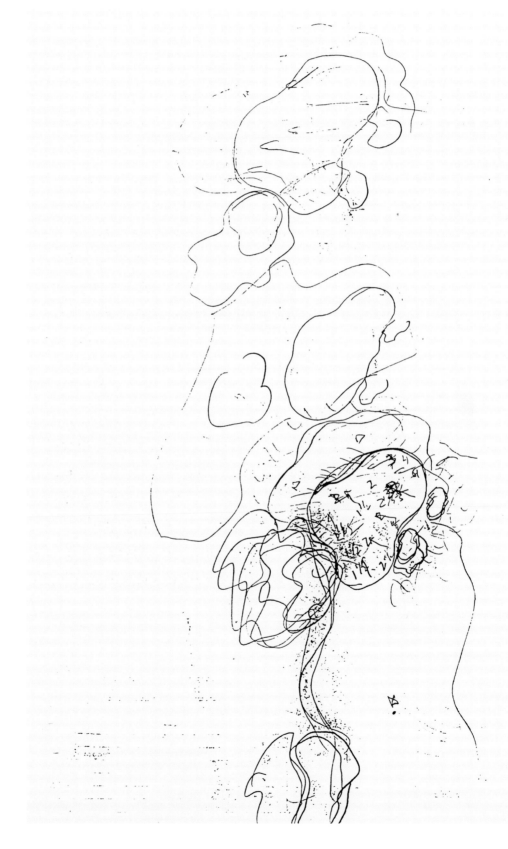

fairway, so if you play it right of the bunker, the fairway runs away from you. If you play it over the bunker on the left, the fairway will run to the left, giving you a better angle into the green.

The green is protected from the right side, and it slopes from right to left and front to back. You have a little false front in the front of the green, two bunkers on the right, one bunker on the left, and one bunker behind. If the pin is on the right side of the green and you're playing downwind, it affords you the opportunity to carry that 240-yard bunker without a real big shot. A lot of players can probably do it with a 3-wood. That gives you a nice angle to get into the green. If you play it out to the right with the wind at your back and the pin in the back right, you can never play it to the hole, because the ball will never stop. The best you can do is go for the center of the green. If the wind shifts into your face, you can decide not to try to force it over the bunker. You can play instead to the right of it with a shorter club and have a slightly longer shot into the green (it's usually going to be less than 130 yards), but the wind in your face will help you stop the golf ball. It's a really neat hole.

While a lot of my design inspirations come from holes that I've played many times, particularly in major championships, the idea for the 12th at The Bear's Club came from a hole that I've only played once: the 15th hole at Rhode Island Country Club. I played it in the summer of 2000 in a charity event staged by PGA Tour members Brad Faxon and Billy Andrade. The course was designed in 1911 by Donald Ross, and while the original Ross hole requires a longer shot into a larger green, I liked the strategy of it. It stuck with me, and I incorporated it into a shorter, somewhat smaller version.

4. How will it look?

When you set out on a picnic, do you go to the dump? Of course not. You look for a pretty place that gets you in touch with nature. A golf course ought to be a pleasant and visually appealing place to spend a day, too. The setting, and how the course is placed into that setting so that the two complement one another, is vitally important. A well-designed course really can't be separated from its surroundings—it's part of them.

In designing a golf course, it's critically important to infuse the course with the surroundings and vice versa. You have to look at the mountains, the vegetation, the lakes, the indigenous grasses—see what you've got and try to bring that through in the finished layout. That tying of what you might call the themes or rhythms of the land into the design is what separates an ordinary golf course from a beautiful one.

If I'm working in a mountain setting, I'll try to mirror the forms of the surrounding mountains in the mounding on the course. I'm not trying to replicate the mountains, and most players don't even notice it on a conscious level, but it's a technique that allows the course to fit in, to match. It's not unlike matching a shirt and tie (said the colorblind course designer). Basically, when you match clothes, you're picking out common themes that make the clothes "go" together.

If I'm working in an area where stands of trees dominate the backdrops, I'll try to reflect the line formed by the tops of trees into, say, the topline at the back of the green. Even in an area that has few cues, such as the desert, I try to bring the rhythm and flow of the land itself into the design.

For example, the 5th hole at the PGA West private course is a par-4 down into a valley. If you look closely at the mounding we did there, you'll see that it gives the impression that the distant surroundings are brought back into the golf course. It mirrors the mountains in the backdrop.

If I'm doing a course on the ocean, I try to bring the ocean and the coastal vegetation through the golf course so that the course blends thoroughly with its surroundings. For instance, at Ocean Hammock in Palm Coast, Florida, we were required to stop construction within a certain distance of the Atlantic coast because of the natural dunes there. But instead of taking our grasses right up to that point, which would have looked abrupt and artificial, we did the opposite. We brought the dunes and their vegetation out into the golf course. We made the dunes look as though they began 100 yards into

Opposite: PGA West, Private Course, La Quinta, California. Hole 5, par-4. Great golf holes and great golf courses mesh not only with their immediate surroundings, but also with their broader environment. The mounding and scalloping we did here at PGA West bring the mountain into the hole.

Overleaf: Ocean Hammock Dunes, Palm Coast, Florida. Hole 9, par-4. Here we came up with a terrific idea for building great golf holes in a fragile seaside environment. On the 9th, rather than bring the golf course to the dunes, we brought dunes to the course.

the golf course, and that way we tied nature into the look and feel and even the playability of the course.

I designed Ocean Hammock in 1999. A year or so later I went to a gathering of the American Society of Golf Course Architects. I heard someone quote one of the great architects as saying that "one of the fundamentals of golf course design is to be able to re-create your surroundings." Over the years, I've read similar quotes from architects like C.B. Macdonald, who wrote: "Glaring artificiality of any kind detracts from the fascination of the game." Alister Mackenzie, who designed Augusta National, Cypress Point, Pasatiempo, and did the routing for both the Scarlet and Gray Courses at my alma mater, Ohio State University, said: "A course should have beautiful surroundings, and all the artificial features should have so natural an appearance that a stranger is unable to distinguish them from nature itself." I feel that if, in the end, a golf course architect doesn't feel that connection instinctively, it's unlikely he'll be able to achieve it in his or her designs.

When we talk about aesthetics and golf course design, I'm reminded of a true story. I was at an outing at a new golf course a few years ago (I'll leave the course and designer unnamed). I did an instructional clinic for the invited guests in the morning. Then all the guests went out and played the course with a group of professionals. Although I didn't play the golf course, I did join them all for dinner afterwards. The service in the clubhouse was terrific. The view from the porch was delightful. The dining room and the appointments were beautiful. The food was delectable. Afterwards, virtually every amateur said: "Man, what an experience. One of the best golf courses I've ever played."

Every pro said: "This may be the worst golf course I've ever seen."

What does that mean? It tells me that when the average golfer heads out for a day of golf, he is not 100 per cent focused on the golf course alone. He likes it well conditioned, he likes it pretty, he likes good service, an enjoyable round, and a great day. The pro or the scratch player bypasses all the peripherals and goes right to the golf: What kind of golf shots do we have, how fair is it, and what kinds of challenges am I being faced with?

I think most modern designers cater very well to one of those two groups. But in order to please the greatest number of people, including my own tastes, I try to meld aesthetics and strategy (good golf shots) in every course I do.

3 Great Golf Holes

I don't think there's anything really new in golf course design. We've been designing and redesigning golf courses for something like 500 years, and I think we've pretty much covered it all. A modern golf course designer's skill lies in his ability to know his client and his customer, and adapt the course not only to those factors, but also to the environment. And, most important of all in my opinion, a course designer has to really understand the game of golf and how it is played by all different levels of golfers.

I've used certain strategies or shots on a hole and forgotten all about them, and five years later I'll play a course that's new to me and see that, given a similar setting and objective, I used the same solution. And I can still play the old links courses of Scotland and find something I hadn't seen before. Sometimes I'll even notice a concept that I thought I originated, only to realize it had been done more than a century ago.

North Berwick Golf Club, North Berwick, Scotland. Hole 15, par-3. This is the original Redan Hole. The concept, perfected by Davie Strath in the mid-nineteenth century, has been replicated countless times by modern-day golf course designers.

That explains how the truly classic golf holes have endured. Take the redan hole. The redan has existed for hundreds of years and there are probably thousands of them in use around the world. The word "redan" actually means a fortification, surrounded on three sides. When applied to a golf hole, a redan is a par-3 with a very deep bunker along one side of the green (usually the left side), more trouble to the opposite side/front that offers a narrow passageway in front, and a green that slopes from front to back. Because the green runs away from the player, the classic redan calls for a low draw that hits short of the green and rolls onto the putting surface (obviously, in a reverse redan you'd play a fade). Behind the green, the redan hole typically has a hollow or a bunker, leaving those who fly the green with a difficult uphill play back to the pin. The strategy of the redan hole is to make the player do something other than fly the ball to the pin. It's the opposite of what today is often called "target golf," in that it demands land-based rather than aerial

Superstition Mountain Golf and Country Club, Prospector Course. Superstition Mountain, Arizona. Hole 17, par-3. This is a good example of a modern-day redan that I've worked on. The only difference between this hole and a pure redan is that instead of putting a bunker in the front/right of the green, my son Gary and I put in a fairly prominent nob. Gary and I codesigned Superstition Mountain. The 2002 Tradition was played on this course.

Spring Creek Ranch, Collierville, Tennessee. Hole 8, par-3. I designed this redan recently. The original Redan Hole green at North Berwick slopes from right to left, but it is not unusual for golf course designers to reverse the concept.

tactics. You don't play to the pin, you play to the high side of the green and let the ball feed toward the pin.

In order to demonstrate the link between ancient and modern golf course design, I've taken two redan holes—the original, the par-3 15th at North Berwick in Scotland and some modern-day redans from among my designs. Certainly there are small differences, but the strategies are the same.

Take the 17th hole at the Prospector course at Superstition Mountain in the town of the same name in Arizona. (I codesigned the course with my son Gary.) It's a traditional redan in that it plays right to left. With tees at 141, 164, and 192 yards, we have a deep bunker on the left and the high section of the green on the right. Unlike a lot of redans, there is no bunker on the front of the high side, there is just a high nob. If you hit through the green, you end up in a deep hollow that's cut to fairway height, so you can putt the ball back up to the green. It's a tough putt or chip.

The 8th hole at Spring Creek Ranch in Collierville, Tennessee, is a reverse redan, meaning it plays left-to-right. It has a bunker on the left-front corner, a big, deep bunker on the right, and a green that slopes classically from front to back and left-to-right. A ball that runs from the front left of the green will trickle down to a position near the back right where a pin would typically be placed. It has a little less pitch to the green than the hole at Prospector, but it's a really nice example of redan theory in action.

We've shown that the modern golf course is a descendant of its forefathers and that there are keys to greatness—that holes designed in the last 50 years are likely to have something in common with great holes designed 150 years ago. However, that still leaves us with the question: What makes a golf hole a *great* golf hole?

Great Par-3s

Several things make a great par-3. Foremost among them is the setting. The most talked-about par-3 I've done in recent years is the 3rd hole at The Four Seasons at Punta Mita in Mexico, "The Ocean par-3." There's no other true island par-3 that I know of on the Pacific Coast. So, visually, a hole like this is hard to beat, and that's primarily what you're looking for in a great par-3. Besides that, it's got terrific strategic elements. It plays 190 yards from the back tees, the prevailing wind is at least slightly in your face, so for me it's a 4-iron, maybe a 3-iron into a stiffer breeze.

From the front tees it plays about 155 yards. It's got a bail-out on a little fairway pad to the right, a bunker to the left. It's a beautiful hole. Now, no architect is going to be blessed with ocean views and Pacific breezes for every par-3 he designs. So, aside from drop-dead aesthetics, what makes a great par-3? Simple: It has to have a variety of ways to play the hole for the variety of people who play it, and it has to stand the test of time.

I think the 12th hole at Muirfield Village is another great example. Same for the 12th hole at Augusta. They may not be set against roaring coastline, but they're undeniably lovely to look at and they require guts to play them. They're not long, so strength is not an issue, and they're not impossible, so anybody can play them. They simply require the ability to fit the ball onto a green that can be played left-to-right or right-to left under differing conditions.

Muirfield Village's 12th can be played in low or played in high. When you're playing to the left, you hit it over the water, but beware of the back bunker. If you're playing to the right, you've got to hit it over the water and over the bunker, but you can't bail left. All kinds of things can happen to you, depending on your choice. You have semisafe ways to play, and some not so safe.

Same with the 12th at Augusta. You've got a semisafe way to play it—directly over the bunker—if you can hit that shot. You can gamble all you want or be as conservative as you want. You can also be penalized accordingly, and you've got to make that decision.

I think the little 7th hole at Pebble Beach is a great little par-3. When they put the pin in the right/back, you've got to make up your mind whether you're going to challenge the ocean and the bunkers or just put the ball in the middle of the green and try to make 3.

I think the 5th at Pebble is also a beautiful little par-3. I've said many times that Pebble Beach is my favorite golf course, so I was delighted when the Pebble Beach Company asked me to restore a few holes prior to the 1992 U.S. Open. In early 1996, they asked me to design a new 5th hole. From the uphill, blind par-3 they'd always had, it was to become a downhill par-3 running along the ocean, with the green set into the cliff that edges the 6th fairway. The idea was to get back to the original intent of the founder, Samuel F.B. Morse. If you look at his memoirs, you'll see that Morse intended to use as much oceanfront land for the golf course as he could, but a local family owned the land on which Morse and his designer, Jack Neville (assisted by Douglas S. Grant), had plotted the 5th hole. For decades the family had refused to sell their land, so Neville was forced to take the course up and around the precious lot. That's the only reason the old 5th ever played inland in the first place.

Even though we were following Morse's intent, we were very careful. Changing Pebble Beach is a little like adjusting the smile on the Mona Lisa. We consulted very carefully with the California Coastal Commission and all of the appropriate environmental agencies. We matched the new bunkers to the existing style, and we matched the old green in size—just under 4,000 square feet.

In the 2000 U.S. Open, the new 5th hole played the toughest hole on the golf course. I didn't design it to be so tough, but the USGA put rough on the left side of the green, which I had designed as the bail-out/run-up option. They took the playability out of the hole. I used the bail-out as a feed-in onto the green. If you use the terrain, you can feed the ball right into the hole. Playing into the back part of the green, you've either got to hit the ball right into the back or play to the front part of the green and putt it back. You've got a variety of different options in how you can play the hole. It can be left to right, right to left. It can be played low, it can be played high, depending on your thinking. If you do what the USGA did by taking away the left-side bounce-in, it turns into the monster it was during the 2000 Open.

I'm very pleased with the way this hole turned out. I think the critics are too. In 2001, Pebble Beach bypassed Pine Valley as the No. 1-ranked golf course in the country. Although the owners of Pebble have been kind enough to credit our design for the 5th

Four Seasons Golf Club, Punta Mita, Mexico. Hole 3B, par-3. Hydration, drainage, and fertilization for this stunning island par-3 are completely self-contained.

Overleaf pages 94 and 95: Muirfield Village Golf Club, Dublin, Ohio. Hole 12, par-3. The 12th at Muirfield Village is only 163 yards long, but it offers the golfer—tour player and member both— a variety of options.

Overleaf page 96 and 97: Augusta National Golf Club, Augusta, Georgia. Hole 12, par-3. The best-known par 3 in the world may well be Jones and Mackenzie's 12th at Augusta. Since 1934, its mixture of swirling winds, slick green, and abundant hazards has challenged and enchanted the best players in the world.

Pebble Beach Golf Links,
Pebble Beach, California.
Hole 5, par-3. My design
of this hole fulfilled the
original plans of Samuel
F.B. Morse, Jack Neville,
and Douglas Grant.

Muirfield Village Golf Club, Dublin, Ohio. Hole 4, par-3. Any green, be it a par-3, -4, or -5, must be designed to accept the shots demanded of the golfer. This green can handle the relatively low trajectory of the long-iron tee shot it demands. A longer hole would require a larger, deeper green.

Overleaf: The Bear's Club, Jupiter, Florida. Hole 2, par-3. Longer par-3s such as this 234-yarder warrant the inclusion of more options. A tee-ball that comes up short here is fine. Conversely, the more aggressive your tee shot, the greater the risk.

hole, I think a lot of the credit has to go back to Morse, Neville, and Grant and their vision. I'm just happy to have had a role in realizing it.

The green complex and what you can do with it depends on the length of the par-3 in question. Take the 4th at Muirfield Village, which measures about 200 yards. It's a very compact green site: a fairly narrow green and severe penalties await balls missed on the wrong side. That kind of demanding green complex wouldn't be fair at 220 yards. It's too tough. For a 220-yard shot, you have open it up. Let's look at a longish par-3 I've done. No. 2 at The Bear's Club is a long par-3, 234 yards from the back. There's water, but set 60 yards away from the green, it's effectively not in play. This is a hole where if you're short of the green there's a place to play and it's a safe area and it's not a bad approach. The more you challenge the hole, though, the more difficult it plays. If the hole is short, the designer shouldn't really offer many options, he should just force the player to play the hole. As the hole gets longer, you have to create more outs, more options, and more variety. If the hole gets really long, you have got to be really fair.

Cabo del Sol, Ocean Course. Cabo San Lucas, Mexico. Hole 17, par-3. The majestic setting on the Baja Peninsula called out for this eye-catching hole.

Great Par-4s

I think when you discuss par-4s, you've got to break them down into long ones, middle ones, and short ones. I've always thought some of the great short par-4s in the world are like the 10th at Riviera Country Club in Los Angeles, a wonderful hole, or the 11th at Merion. Not a great tee shot there, but a wonderful little second shot. Short par-4s need to be very demanding.

A great par-4 has to require the following: one good shot to make par and two good shots to make birdie. Take the 14th at Muirfield Village. That's a wonderful little short par-4. You can play a driver off the tee, challenge the creek with distance on the left, and leave yourself with a sand wedge to the green, or you can lay back off the tee and the second shot becomes the challenge. You've got to take a gamble on either the first shot or the second one.

The 10th at Riviera is similar. You can gamble with the tee shot and try to take it into the green, or you can take an iron out to the left and play a little longer second shot up the channel.

I think that on a longer par-4 you have to be more forgiving, particularly around the green. Take the 3rd hole at Castle Pines. Like a lot of my golf holes, there's ample room off the tee, or you can gamble your way across the barranca. If you get it across the barranca, you've got a shorter shot in and an easier angle. It's a longer shot from the other side and a tougher angle, but both times you've got plenty of bail-out. In order to really score, you need precision on either the first or second shot.

We made some changes at Muirfield Village's 6th hole for the 2000 Memorial Tournament. It's now a much better par-4. I took out the tree and put in some fairway on the right as a bounce-in (mostly for the membership). Then, on the tee-shot I put a fairway bunker on the right, down about 300 yards on the knob, and enlarged the green on the left around the water.

Here, you've got options off the tee. You can lay up short of the fairway bunker and have a little longer second. You can drive it into the narrow part of the fairway and play a shorter iron over the water. You've got the option to play the ball to the right of the green and bounce the ball in. On the approach, you can carry it in, you can draw it in, you can use the terrain. You have multiple ways to make the hole work. I try not to box somebody in so that there's only one way to play the hole, especially if it's a long hole. When it's a short hole, I'll offer fewer ways to play it, in order to make the player be more precise.

I get a little more flexible on mid-length par-4s. Take the 18th at Muirfield Village. That's a good example of the way I go about designing such holes. There you can squeeze a driver out, have maybe an 8-iron into the green. Or you can take a 3-wood, which most of us do, into the fat of the fairway, but then you're left with a 4- or 5-iron into the green, a tougher second shot. The 2nd at Muirfield is also a good mid-length par-4.

Sometimes I like to have a mid to long par-4 followed by a very short par-4. When I do, it often creates a symbiotic relationship between the holes. Take the 12th and 13th holes at Valhalla. No. 12 is a big, strong hole requiring a driver and a good middle iron into a very difficult green. If you play that hole well, make par or better, all of a sudden the 13th, a very short par-4, gives you the opportunity to make a pretty big move in both score and momentum in just two holes. You think, "If I can make a par at 12, I've a got a good chance for birdie at 13. I could really make something happen here." However, if you bogey 12, it pressures you to play 13 well, and under pressure that water around the green looms a little larger. I like to pair up holes that way sometimes, and sometimes I'll do the reverse—put the easier hole first—but the effect of the tandem is the same. Success or failure on the one can dictate your play on the other.

Now, I've said for years and just about every player knows that you can only play one shot at a time. When I'm on the golf course, I'm only thinking about the shot at hand. But before I tee it up, particularly in a competition, I've thought out most of the holes. I've thought about how I'm going to try to play the round, what I can expect where. I've mapped out the risks and the opportunities. By juxtaposing a hole like the 12th with a hole like the 13th, I give the golfer something to think about at a key point in the round. Particularly in tournament play, these duos force a player to be a little stronger on the first of the holes because he knows that the field is likely to pick up a shot on the next one.

Another good example of the relationship between consecutive holes is the 17th and 18th holes at Glen Abbey in Ontario. They run right next to each other but in opposite

Overleaf: Muirfield Village Golf Club, Dublin, Ohio. Hole 14, par-4. This 363-yard hole makes a player gamble early or late.

Castle Pines Golf Club, Castle Rock, Colorado. Hole 3, par-4 (shown both in the photo and my sketch). This 462-yarder is a particularly beautiful example of a risk-reward hole. The key to it, both visually and strategically, is the barranca that meanders up the fairway.

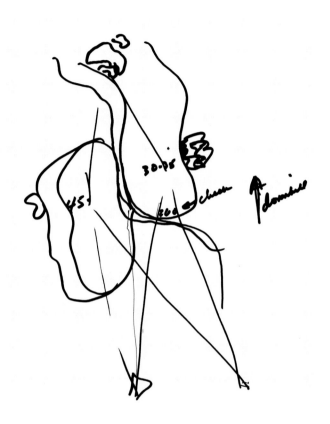

directions. The 17th is a par-4. If the wind is blowing out of the southeast, the 17th won't play particularly long, but the par-5 18th will. In September, which is when the course used to host the Canadian Open, they'll often have a northwest wind up there. In that case, 17 will play tough and 18 becomes a short par-5, so we put water in front of the green to keep the 18th from playing too easily downwind.

It gets back to balance, the single most important element in a golf course design. Oddly enough, some great courses lack it. I've said that Pebble Beach is my favorite place to play golf, but even it sometimes lacks balance. That's because when you're playing along the streak of ocean holes—6, 7, 8, 9, 10—and the wind is blowing from the south, you can get absolutely hammered. Every one of those holes plays into the ocean wind. There's no relief; it's just a relentless trek. The south wind is the storm wind, so if you can be strong on 6, 7, 8, 9, and 10, you'll be rewarded by playing the backside downwind. Pebble Beach is a hard course to achieve balance on because of where it is, but you trade the lack of balance for that gorgeous stretch of ocean holes. Most links courses will go out on one wind and back on another.

It's the same thing at St. Andrews, another of my favorite golf courses, and one of the world's most beloved links. The front nine there goes out largely in one direction and then the back nine runs back to the clubhouse in the opposite direction. You could have calm conditions for the front, get a light breeze at your back for a little help coming home, and you'd have St. Andrews licked. If the wind is blowing hard all day, it's going to be tough one way and easy the other. But it's that relentlessness of playing six or seven holes in a row in one direction that makes it different from most of the courses we build today. Today we try to balance the wind as we design the course.

I have the same problem with one of my own golf course designs. Bear Lakes (The Lakes Course) is a project we did in West Palm Beach, Florida, in the mid-1980s. It was a very linear piece of property. The shape of the land forced us to go essentially straight out and then straight back. It's a good golf course, but it doesn't quite achieve the balance you'd ideally like to have. Sometimes the land just forces your hand. St. Andrews is similarly constrained. It's bounded closely by the village on one side and the Firth of Forth on the other. Originally, of course, the land there was just a meadow for grazing animals, but when Allan Robertson upgraded the links in the 1800s he had no

*Above and left:
Muirfield Village
Golf Club, Dublin,
Ohio. Hole 18, par-4.
It looks graceful today,
but it took a lot of work
to get this hole and the
clubhouse into their
current positions.*

Valhalla Golf Club,
Louisville, Kentucky.
Hole 12, par-4. No hole
is played in a vacuum.
That is why I will some-
times pair a difficult
par-4, like this 467-
yarder . . .

. . . with a comparatively easy one, like the 384-yard 13th.

room to work with. He didn't deviate much from the original out-and-back direction of the routing, but even if he'd wanted to, he didn't have that option. There was nowhere else to go. Of course, St. Andrews is still one of the great golf courses in the world. I guess it's safe to say that if Pebble and St. Andrews have imperfections, then there will never be a perfect golf course.

Glen Abbey Golf Club,
Oakville, Ontario. Hole
17, par-4. Like the 12th
and 13th at Valhalla, the
17th and 18th holes at
Glen Abbey have a
symbiotic relationship.

Above: Glen Abbey Golf Club, Oakville, Ontario. Hole 18, par-5. By design, if the wind was with you on the 17th, it will be in your face on the 18th.

Left: Sketch of the original holes 17 and 18 at Glen Abbey.

Great Par-5s

Most of my golf courses have one par-5 that's largely unreachable in two. I say largely because if it's 100 percent unreachable 100 percent of the time, that can make the hole a little boring. A. W. Tillinghast's 17th hole on Baltusrol's Lower Course, one of the great holes in all of golf, is the model for most of the long par-5s I design.

With most par-5s, if you hit a bad tee shot, the thinking is to chop a 6-iron out of the rough and you still have a chance to get home in three. The Baltusrol Lower Course 17th hole (630-yards during the 1993 U.S. Open) rules out that sort of thinking. It features what I call a "multiple-effect penalty." The cross bunkers are out there about 325 yards off the tee. If you happen to drive the ball into the rough, particularly in heavy U.S. Open rough, or drive it into one of the short bunkers off the tee, you won't be able to carry the cross bunkers on your second shot. So, if you're short of the bunkers in two, there's no way you're going to reach the green in three. It's just too far. You're forced to lay up again, short of the hazards in front of the green, and then play your chip up to the green.

The complaint I hear about a lot of long par-5s is that they require two boring shots. The beauty of the 17th at Baltusrol is that it's a long par-5 where both of the first two shots are quite intense. You miss either one and you're pretty much assured of bogey or worse. Although it's more penal than most long par-5s, I think that it's a great model. It's a real marathon. If you make a mistake, the next problem is compounded. I use that a lot. For example, I used it on the Colleton River 10th.

I like to have one or two par-5s that are sort of in-between, reachable by perhaps 30 percent of all players depending on conditions. And then I like to have a third par-5 that's reachable by most strong players most of the time. These three variations give the golf course a nice blend.

I have to be a little more liberal with the long 5s, that is, allow more room for error. The "tweeners" can be a little more demanding, and the shorter 5s—the ones you can reach all the time—have to be more demanding and more penal.

The 18th hole on the Cochise Course at Desert Mountain is a good example of my thinking on short par-5s (see page 166). At 511 yards, it's not very long. Good players are going to birdie it most of the time, but you've got to be very careful with your sec-

ond shot: If you hit it short, you end up in the wash. Hit it long and you end up in a greenside bunker, playing out to a green that slopes away and down toward the wash. That's a very, very difficult up-and-down.

I love the 13th hole at Augusta. It's one of my favorite par-5s. For most of my career it was 465 yards (with the recent revision, it now measures more like 495 yards), a short and not very difficult three-shot hole. But if you're going for the green in two, the first and second shots have to be extremely precise.

Colleton River Plantation, Bluffton, South Carolina. Hole 10, par-5. This long par-5, nicknamed "Baltusrol," is loosely modeled on A.W. Tillinghast's 17th hole at the legendary U.S. Open venue.

*Both pages: Baltusrol
Golf Club, Springfield,
New Jersey, Lower Course.
Hole 17, par-5. I think
the 17th at Baltusrol is
the gold standard for
"unreachable" par-5s.*

4 The Tournament Courses

In my 30 years in the design business, I've designed over 200 golf courses in 26 countries. I've worked in just about every climate that can grow grass. I've designed courses at altitudes over 9,000 feet and below sea level. But of all those projects, my best-known designs are the courses that host professional tournaments and other significant championships. By hosting important events, our designs are recognized as superior layouts. Just as important, they are put to the test by some of the best players in the world. I'm proud of the fact that from 1973 to the end of 2001, 62 Nicklaus-designed golf courses had hosted a total of 350 professional tournaments.

Although we don't have room to detail all 62 of those courses, I thought it might be interesting to take an in-depth look at some of my best-known tournament courses, to show how these projects came about and explain some of the thinking that went into them.

Harbour Town Golf
Links, Hilton Head
Island, South Carolina.
Hole 13, par-5. I con-
sulted on the design of
Harbour Town, but the
wooden planks that out-
line the bunker were
Alice Dye's idea.

Harbour Town

Harbour Town is without doubt the best known of the golf courses on which Pete Dye and I collaborated. Charles Fraser asked us to create a resort golf course, and Pete and I were about halfway through construction in June of 1969 when Charles came back and said, "Oh, by the way, we're going to host the PGA Tour Heritage Classic here in November."

Until that day, we had no idea we were designing a tournament course. As I said earlier, knowing who is going to play your course and knowing what purpose it will serve—public recreation, resort enjoyment, member satisfaction, or professional competition—dictates your design strategy. So you'd think that would change everything. Well, we didn't have time to change everything. They needed a course for the Heritage Classic and they got one. We rye-grassed the golf course so it would grow in quickly, and that's basically what they played the first Heritage Classic on.

Obviously, I didn't know much about golf course design at that time. Pete did most of the design work on Harbour Town. Pete's wife, Alice, contributed several holes and I contributed a few. The course was a lesson in small greens. It's set in typical South Carolina Low Country and I wouldn't really have known the first thing to do if it had not been for Pete and Alice. It's not a long golf course at 6,900 yards, but it's very demanding. Still, it's been very popular over the years, not only with PGA Tour players, but also with amateurs who vacation in Hilton Head.

As I said, I was involved in almost all the holes, but I didn't have a great deal to do with the overall design. But Hilton Head is significant to me as the place where I started to think strategically. A good example is the 2nd hole. It's a par-5, but you play it out to the right and there are trees on the right side of the green and a bunker in front, so it's hard to get to the green. On the tee shot, you have a bunker on the left. The closer you play your drive to that bunker or over that bunker, the better the hole sets up your angle to the green.

On the 4th hole, a par-3, there's water on the left and a bail-out on the right, and we started thinking about how to make the bail-out so that it was playable but difficult. So the green is pitched to the water to leave you with a tough chip.

For the green complex on the 7th hole, Pete pointed out a handful of trees and said, "Well, what do you see here?" I said, "I just see a green surrounded by sand." That's what we did. We made an island green in the sand. That's the way Pete and I worked. I'd make a suggestion and he'd say, "O.K., let's look at that." If it didn't work when we saw it roughed out, we tried something else. We'd think out loud, sketch it in the dirt, put it on paper, add a few finishing details, and that was it. It was fun. I really enjoyed working with Pete. The important lesson to me was that out of essentially nothing, you can really create something great. With Pete, I learned how to use my imagination, to visualize the elements of a potential golf hole or golf course and then make those elements fit. That was a very valuable lesson for me.

We were kicking around ideas for the 9th hole. We had already pretty much decided that it would be a short par-4 (a personal favorite). When I looked at the area planned for the green, I thought we needed a bunker in back. Then I thought, "Why don't we put in a bunker and build the green in a U-shape around it?" I'm happy to report that that green, even after the recent remodeling, is still there.

Since the first time he used them (on the par-4 13th at The Golf Club at New Albany), Pete has become famous—or infamous—for using wooden planks. The funny thing is that the famous cypress-wood boards at the 13th at Harbour Town weren't even his idea. They weren't mine either, they were actually suggested by Alice. In addition to having been a world-class amateur competitor (seven Indiana Women's Amateur titles, three Florida State Women's Amateur titles, five Women's Western Senior Open titles, two U.S. Women's Senior Amateur titles, and membership on the 1970 Curtis Cup team), Alice has superb golf course design skills. She has worked with Pete on dozens of designs, and is one of only three female members of the American Society of Golf Course Architects. The cypress boards were her idea. In fact, Pete joked about that with me recently. The owners of Harbour Town completed a restoration of the golf course a year or so back. At the beginning of the restoration, Pete paid a visit to the course. He called and told me that as he walked our 32-year-old design he realized that "the only thing that didn't look dated was the cypress that Alice put in."

The 15th hole was pretty much my idea. It's been changed some since—I think the green was enlarged once—but it was originally a par-5 that we tucked around a corner of the water. I felt that if you're going to bail out, you still ought to be faced with a difficult chip. We made it a 3-shot hole. If you play it back you can play up the length of

Harbour Town Golf Links, Hilton Head, South Carolina. Hole 15, par-5. The 15th at Harbour Town is one of the first holes that was essentially my own. The idea was to make it a three-shot hole, but to maintain some emphasis on the third shot. A chip shot to a right pin here can be deadly. Some alterations were made in the redesign, but the hole plays the same way.

the green. If you hit the green, fine. If you miss the green to the right and find the bunker, you aren't too badly off. If you miss the bunker to the right, you are still in the fairway but have a pitch over the bunker with the green running away from you.

I've used that concept for years, and I think it's a wonderful one. Forty years later, I used the same thinking (only in reverse) in designing the 10th hole at The Bear's Club.

Muirfield Village Golf Club

In 1966, I was playing in the Masters and my wife, Barbara, and I were spending some time with an old friend of mine, Ivor Young, and his wife, Carol. We marveled at Augusta National, saying how great it would be to do something like what Bobby Jones did there, but to do it in Columbus, Ohio, where I grew up. The idea was not so much to repeat Augusta National, the golf course, as it was to replicate Augusta National, the experience.

Ivor's business was real estate, so after he got back to Columbus he started scouting out potential sites with the understanding that I'd come look at them when I had time. He rounded up 10 or 11 different sites over the next few months, but as it turns out the Flowers family property, the first site we visited, a 160-acre plot that I used to hunt on as a kid, is the first one we bought.

Over four or five years we accumulated more than 1,600 acres of prime real estate, and while I was doing well financially, the carrying costs of this acreage became a significant drain on my resources. There were times when we seriously considered ditching the project. The "experts" told us that we needed to have land surrounding the course so that we could sell homes, and that those home sales would make the golf course viable. We did that—Muirfield Village is a great community—but if I were to do it all over again, I would build the golf course, retain a pristine perimeter around the course for spectator parking, and never build a house. That just was not financially practical at the time.

Just as it became clear that I was going to have to find a way to finance the project, along came Put Pierman. I had known Put vaguely in my high-school days, but he was referred to me by Ivor as someone who might be able to help. Put, a contractor, financed a portion of the project and arranged additional financing in 1971 through The Ohio Company, which did a $9-million public offering. Of that, $2.6 million was for the golf course and the clubhouse. Today, you'd need more than double that just for the course. We started construction in 1972 and promptly spent $2.4 million on the golf course alone. The clubhouse could wait.

We knew from the beginning that we were looking for a solid test of golf that would challenge the best players in the world. In fact, one of the first people to see the property was the late Joe Dey. Joe was a very dear friend and a man I respected enor-

*Muirfield Village
Golf Club, Dublin,
Ohio, today.*

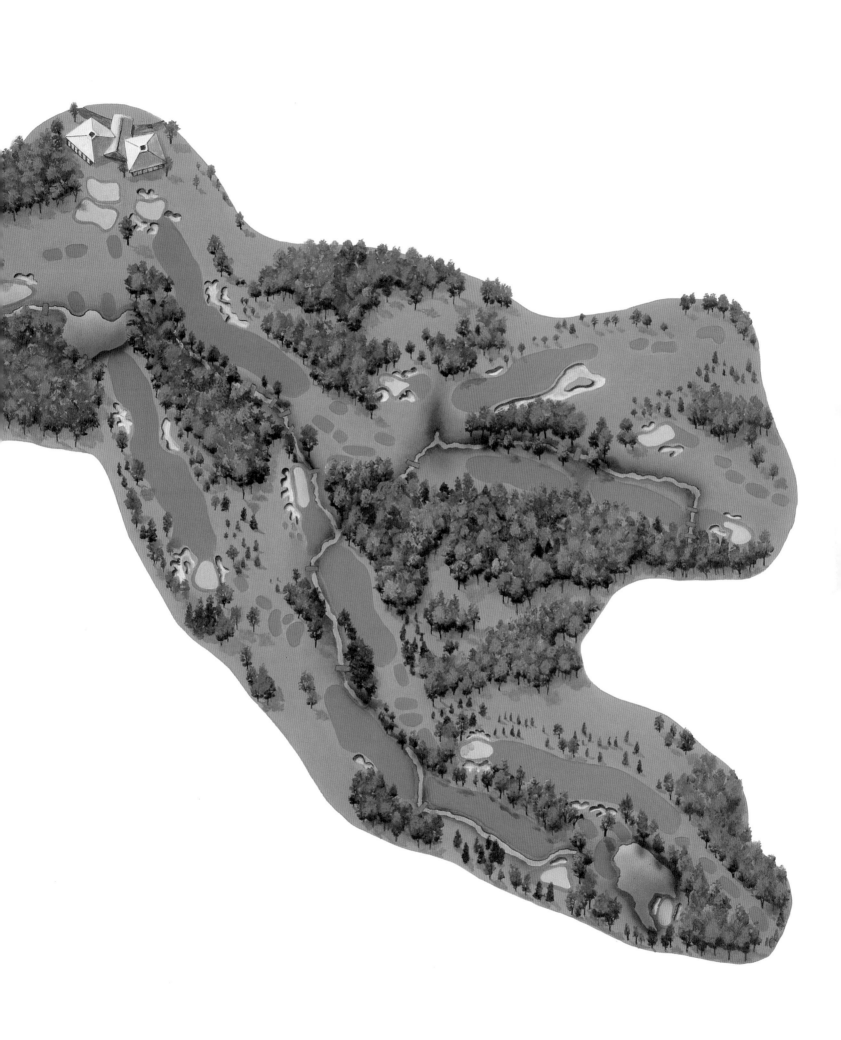

mously. He was the executive director of the USGA from 1964 to 1969. He then became the first commissioner of the PGA Tour (when it split from the PGA of America) from 1969 to 1974. He had a huge impact on my life not only as an administrator, but also as a counselor, a confidant, and a friend. I knew we wanted a significant event for our course, but it was largely Joe who generated the concepts that make the Memorial Tournament unique: The Captain's Club and the honoree. Both emerged from conversations we had. He's the one who said that if we "paid our dues" by sponsoring the Ohio Kings Island Open for a few years, we might then be able to bring our own tournament to Columbus. We did, and we got the tournament.

The course is laid out on gently rolling terrain that slopes from west to east toward the Scioto River, with a couple of streams running through it. With the prevailing wind coming from the west, about half your round at Muirfield Village is downhill/downwind and the other half is into the wind (what wind there is in the Columbus area). Although a little uphill, it plays as if it were downhill. Overall, it's an exquisite site for a golf course.

One of things we try to do at a site such as Muirfield is to blend the natural elements such as streams, pasture, woods, etc., into the routing and the strategy of the course. We had no shortage of streams to deal with.

We had a stream coming from the north that ran along No. 6 and No. 5, across No. 2, and down No. 3. We had a stream that came from the northwest that ran down 12 and 11 and came in on 14, 18, 1, 2. It tied into another stream at No. 3. We had another stream that came from the west along No. 15 and tied into the one at 18. We had those major streams converging on the property. The land itself was mostly clay under the surface and divided about equally between trees and pasture.

The varied woodland/wetland/pasture topography presented interesting problems, and I was fortunate to have some help. Muirfield was built at the beginning of my association with Desmond Muirhead. Jay Morrish was working for Desmond at the time (he came to work full-time for me after we completed Muirfield). Morrish, who has since had a very successful career first as Tom Weiskopf's design partner and now in business with his own son, was one of the best technicians I've ever seen in the design business. He could take ideas to the field and make them work. From a drainage stand-

Muirfield Village Golf Club, Dublin, Ohio. Hole 6, par-4.

Overleaf: Hole 5, par-5. The convergence of streams on the property was both a challenge and a blessing.

point or in terms of making a bunker work, he was a very good field man. Bob Cupp came to work with me later on and they made a great combination, sort of like Mr. Inside and Mr. Outside. Bob did the drawings and Jay did the execution. Bob understood what would and wouldn't work, and Jay, in the field, knew how to make the idea actually function.

Who's going to play the course? It ends up being an issue of balance. That balance largely escaped me in my formative design years. If at Kings Island we went completely in favor of the public course player, at Muirfield I went completely in the opposite direction. That's when I started to learn about designing a golf course that allows the average member to enjoy his weekly test while presenting the better player with a serious challenge. I've since made many, many changes to make Muirfield fairer and more enjoyable for the membership.

Most courses are built for their membership and then adjusted for tournaments. Muirfield was done exactly the opposite. That means that over the years I've had to make countless small (and not so small) changes to the golf course. I kept adding bailouts—places where the average player or just the more conservative player can play to safely with the thinking that while he may sacrifice his chance at a birdie, he'll minimize his odds of a bogey or worse and have a decent shot at par.

Some adjustments were not even strategic. For instance, when we rebuilt the greens in 1999, we included the whole subsurface. They were originally built to USGA specifications, but back then we didn't know that with calcareous sand the greens would stop percolating. In other words, the roots and sand and dirt sealed so tightly together that no air or water could get in to do their jobs. At the same time, we made some significant design changes. That's when I changed the 5th hole and the 15th hole.

Two years ago, I corrected the strategy on the 5th. Before, you weren't rewarded for two good shots. Now, you are rewarded for a nice tee shot and a nice second shot and you can play up to the green. Before, if you did not hit a good tee shot, you could hit to the weak side of the left fairway and the green opened up a little, but you had to play it over water, which was hard for the members. These holes are now much more user-friendly for the members, and the second shot for the pros is much more difficult. It's a better strategy for the members. The more you put the ball up to the right side, the closer you play it to the bunker, the better angle you have for playing a pitch shot. Or you can take it all the way home, which I've asked the golfers to do. So the holes are the same—I'm just asking the player to do something different.

Also, the original design for No. 7 didn't allow for a bounce-in approach to the green. So three or four years after we opened the course, I put in about a 20-yard area—I call it a fairway pad—for the members to bounce the ball into the green. Over the history of the Memorial Tournament, I've seen quite a few Tour players use the bounce-in.

I made another change on No. 7 in 2000. I had a series of bunkers out there that did not mean anything. There was a bunker out there about 260 yards on the left. I put another one out about 295, and brought it into play in the fairway, right where all the big hitters were driving it in the tournament. Then I made the fairway about 25 yards wide and sloped it. So if you drive the ball well past the bunker and to the right, you're fine. But if you're trying to bomb it and you hit it just past the bunker on the right, you'll go through the fairway and into the rough. If you carry right over the heart of the bunker, you're perfect in the middle of the fairway. It used to be that if you played left you could still kick into the fairway and you had a pretty easy second shot. Now, if you hit it left, I've put rough in there. With the rough there, you could have some problems. From a strategic standpoint, I don't mind guys trying to play left of the bunker, but with these changes they're forced to hit a great shot.

I enlarged the green at No. 8 a few years ago because it was too small. What happens when you have a super-small green is that all the foot traffic occurs over the same area and the green takes a real beating. I enlarged the green on No. 9 after about the fifth year of the Memorial Tournament because it was just too tough for the members (and probably the pros) to play. It's now probably a third bigger than it used to be.

I took out a bunker, but the 10th hole hasn't changed very much over the years. Nor has No. 11. I did lengthen the hole 25 yards from the back tee and I gave the members a bounce-in on the right side that they can use for either the second or third shot. I had two bunkers on the right, and I took out the first. The members were the only ones who were going to hit it there anyway. If the pros were going to hit it in a bunker,

Above and opposite: Hole 7, par-5. Not all changes intended for the members go unnoticed by the Tour professionals. I have seen more than a few Tour players use the fairway pad we installed in front of the 7th green.

Overleaf: Hole 17, par-4. I have been thinking about making some changes here. A well-placed fairway bunker or two will force the long hitters to be accurate.

they were going to put it in the second, about 280 yards off the back tee. And I narrowed the fairway to about 33 yards at that point, to place an extra premium on accuracy.

I enlarged the green on No. 12 for exactly the same reasons as No. 8. Too much traffic, too difficult for the membership. No. 13 has only changed a little. I tried to make it a little tougher for the pros by adding a second bunker on the left.

I changed the bunkers in back of the 14th green. They were impossible. They're still very difficult, but at least at the Stimpmeter speed that the members play they still have a chance. In the tournament, you just can't do anything from back there, it's an absolute bogey unless you're Houdini. I also used to have a bunker short and left of the green that I eliminated because it gave the members so much trouble. I haven't really changed the tee shot or the second shot at 15. I lowered the green a little to make it more visible to the members. You still can't see it perfectly from the fairway, but you can definitely see it better, and I added a bunker short left. No. 16 hasn't changed much.

It's No. 17 that I'm thinking about changing right now. We have the waste bunker that sits to the left of the fairway and runs pretty much the length of the hole. I may take it out and put three smaller bunkers along the left edge of the fairway at about 250, 270, and 290 yards. The existing waste bunker can be grassed and converted into soft little rolls and hollows and some additional gallery access. The new strategy would be that the moderate hitter would have more fairway to play to. The big hitter has never really been too worried about the waste bunker, but now, with the existing bunker on the right at 280 yards off the tee, and the third of the new bunkers across a 25-yard-wide fairway, the big hitter will be forced to find a little control or possibly even throttle back. I think this change will work out better for everybody.

As for the 17th green, we've changed that significantly over the years. It used to run away from you severely, and the members could never play it. It's still not overly easy on the members, but the new design helps them at least keep the ball on or near the green as opposed to rolling off. Lately, I've been thinking about putting a lake there. Make it a shorter hole. Take the tee back. I don't know if I'm going to do it or not. What I think I would probably do is dam up the water in the ravine, pull the green down toward the water, and put in a greenside bunker or two. We already have a very nice amphitheater behind that green and we could make the amphitheater even bigger. That would short-

My sketch on this napkin shows how I envision the new tee shot at the 17th. No one ever said that designers have to be able to draw.

en the hole by about 20 to 25 yards, but I'd leave the members' tees where they are and
pull back the tournament tees. It could make 17 a very exciting hole both in terms of its
potential impact on the outcome of the Memorial Tournament and from the standpoint
of supporting a large gallery.

Finally, at No. 18 I rerouted the stream that now runs outside the trees on the left-hand
side of the hole as you look at the green from your second shot. I brought it a little more
into play by routing it inside the trees. The fairway was about 40 yards wide, and this
reduced it to about 30 yards. A player is forced to decide whether he wants to risk
blasting up to where the stream bounds the left side of a 30-yard-wide fairway. If he's
successful, he has a shortish iron into the green. The other option is to play it safe, short
of where the brook comes into play, but then he's left with a longish iron into the
green. To my mind, such decisions are what the game is all about. With the historic
wins we've had in the last few years, The Memorial Tournament isn't lacking for excite-
ment, but with those changes to 17 and 18, anything could happen down the stretch.
I think they're very nice changes to the golf course.

All that detail can obscure the idea behind Muirfield Village. The idea was to design and build a golf course for tournament golf that would bring the best in golf to Columbus, Ohio, my hometown. Beyond that, we were bringing a fairly radical idea to the table. We were going to build not only a first-rate championship golf course, but we were also intent on building the first golf course that had ever been built with the gallery in mind. This was the birth of what people now refer to as stadium golf. The plan was to have as many amphitheaters as possible.

We tried to create a golf course that the players would like, that would challenge them. We wanted what you'd call a "second-shot golf course," similar to Bobby Jones and Alister MacKenzie's philosophy at Augusta National. That is, when you play the course from the members' tees, you've got plenty of room to drive the ball and you have relatively easy access to the greens. Then, all you do when you want to host a world-class field is hide the pins, cut the greens, and take the tees back, and you end up with a first-rate championship golf course, one that puts the emphasis not on the tee shot, but on the second shot and/or the approach shot (in the case of par-5s).

The 18th at Muirfield has always been an exciting finishing hole. Since the photo on the opposite page was taken, I have rerouted a stream that used to run outside the trees to the left and essentially out of play. It now runs inside the trees and confronts the long-ball hitter with an added challenge.

Glen Abbey

Glen Abbey Golf Club, Oakville, Ontario. Hole 8, par-4. This is one of my favorite holes on the course.

Not long after the completion of Muirfield Village I was contacted by Dick Grimm, who was then the president of the Royal Canadian Golf Association. Dick asked if I'd be interested in designing a golf course that would serve as the permanent home of the Canadian Open. They had the site all set in Oakville, Ontario—in fact, there was an old golf course there. Aside from a stream that ran through a limited low section of the land, it was a pretty bland piece of property on which we could do nearly anything we wanted.

This was my first solo assignment, and I came up with a concept I called a "spoke-and-wheel" design or a "central theme." That is, rather than put the clubhouse at the edge of the golf course, I'd put it right in the middle and build the golf holes to play away from the hub and back. A few holes, the ones we put down in the valley, broke out of the pattern, but the overall effect was like a wagon wheel.

There was method to the madness. The idea behind the "spoke-and-wheel" design was to maximize spectator-friendliness for Canada's premier championship. With this plan, the gallery can literally spend all day within 50 yards of the clubhouse and still see most of the action. Without leaving the hub, they can see portions of the 1st, 2nd, 3rd, and 4th holes. They miss Nos. 5 and 6, but then get No. 7 coming back, and get parts of 8 and all of 9 and 10. They miss the valley holes, which are good golf holes, but then they can see all of 16, 17, and 18. That's without walking very far.

Also, beyond the hub there's an outer hub, which is really a network of cross-walks that allows the more active spectator to see even more golf, but with very little effort compared to most golf courses.

Then I had a beautiful plan for the valley. I was going to clear out some of the trees on the ridge along the 16th fairway and to the left of No. 10, and create an area from which the gallery could see not only Nos. 10 and 16, but all the holes in the low valley section.

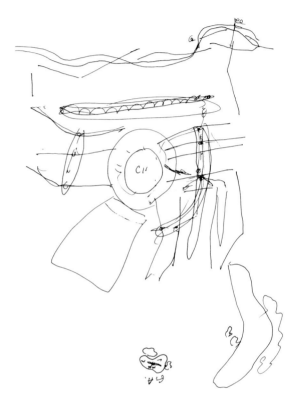

In this rough sketch of my plan for Glen Abbey, you can see that the clubhouse is at the hub of the golf course.

Unfortunately, I could not get environmental approval for that. They wouldn't let me cut enough trees or even limb them up so I could clear a line of sight for the gallery. Had that been approved, the spectator would have had visual access to about 70 percent of the golf course from only a few vantage points. Even so, I'm proud of Glen Abbey. We did some really creative thinking there.

At this point in my career I was confident, but I was still learning and knew that I had a lot to learn. Again, as has been the case throughout my design career, I was fortunate to have some first-rate help. Jay Morrish and Bob Cupp worked for me at the time. From a technical standpoint I was pretty green. In fact, I still am. I've always tried to focus on what I enjoy the most and what I do the best, and that's the design. I rely on real technical experts for putting the technical touches in place.

No. 8 is one of my favorite holes at Glen Abbey. It's a par-4 of about 460 yards on what used to be nothing but open field. We planted the stand of trees to the left and put in a couple of bunkers on the right to guard the dogleg. What I really like is the green complex. There's a bunker front-right and another bunker on the left. We put a ridge in the green, which gave us a high spot in the middle and created a low spot in the front of the green, a medium area to the right, and a medium-high area in back.

At No. 12, I tried to create a little of the feeling you get at the 12th hole at Royal Lytham & St. Annes in Lancashire, England. Lytham, designed in 1896 by George Lowe, Jr., is on the British Open rota. (It's where Bobby Jones won the first of his back-to-back British Open titles in 1926. The second venue, of course, was St. Andrews.) Well, Lytham has a par-3 with a false-front green, and if you hit into that false front the green will feed you into a bunker. That's what I did at Glen Abbey.

No. 17 is also an interesting hole. We were presented with an open field and decided we'd probably put two holes side by side. We had some nice trees on the right. There was an old barn, which is now their maintenance building, and for aesthetic reasons we wanted to play away from that. So what did I do? I created a strategy in which I gave you a carry bunker about 250 yards off the tee. I took the fairway out and around the carry bunker, I then bunkered the left side diagonally from left to right so that the farther you drive the ball, the more you have to play over the bunker and challenge the right trees. If you bail left you'll find a bunker.

Then, I didn't quite know what to do with the green. There's a natural ridge in the area where we were planning to put it and that's when it occurred to me to create a C-shaped green. I created a low green, a middle green, and a high green, and put a bunker in the open space. Why I did it, I don't really know, but it was different, it looked good, and it presented a challenge. It also created an identity for the hole and caused its share of controversy. Sometimes that's not a bad thing. The green has been changed a little over the years, but I think it's still pretty much the same design.

When it came time to do No. 18, coming back alongside 17 but in the opposite direction, I just peppered the area between them with bunkers and put a gallery area right through them. The strategy for the hole was based on the bunkers that play the left-hand side of 17. Only there's one big one that really comes more into play on the left side of 18. That bunker is the cornerstone of the 18th hole.

What I like most about Glen Abbey is the finish. You have two potential eagles in the last three holes. People tend to focus on the water at 18. I would suggest you pay as

much attention to the bunkering that runs behind the 18th green as you do to the water that stands in front. The two have a cause-and-effect relationship. The water forces players to bail out long or left. And if you catch one of those bunkers, you're faced with a downhill shot out of a bunker with water staring you in the face. It's a tough shot.

My relationship with Glen Abbey is interesting. It's the first golf course I designed solo, so it has a special place in my heart. However, it also plays host to one of the few significant national championships I never won.

Above: Hole 18, par-5. On the 18th, it is the water that catches everybody's attention, but for the better player the real issue is the bunker behind the green.

Overleaf: Hole 17, par-4. The 17th is a great example of how a golf hole's surroundings help shape the design. Here we had issues not only with the land, but with an existing structure.

Shoal Creek

I've had a lot of clients who wanted to land a prestigious tournament with their golf courses. Hall Thompson was a little different. He never envisioned hosting a PGA Tour event, much less a major championship. Then, as soon as he did the golf course he was awarded the 1984 PGA Championship. He's since had a U.S. Amateur (1986) and a second PGA in 1990. I think he'd like to host the Tour Championship some day. In fact, there's already been some talk about taking the Tour Championship to Birmingham eventually, and I hope they'll at least consider Shoal Creek.

Shoal Creek began with a call from Hall Thompson. I'd never heard of him, never met him in my life. He said, "Jack, I want to do a golf course in Alabama. I want you to come down and see my property." So I went down and saw his property. It sat between Oak Mountain and Double Oak Mountain. I looked at the land and told him I wasn't sure if I could see a golf course there or not. I'd need to study some topographical maps and other data before I made a decision.

All that was there in 1974 was logging roads winding through the hills. I told him he had a lot of par-3s on his land, but I wasn't sure he had what was needed for an 18-hole golf course. So Jay and Bob and I went back to the office and got to work on a routing. In those days, we each did our own individual routing. Then we'd create a composite, and from that we'd arrive at the final draft. Nowadays, I have my staff do the early routing, primarily because they're superbly talented, but also because most golf course design work these days has a real-estate component to it. I let the staff figure out that part with the developer, then they do a preliminary routing and work on it from there. Very rarely does a routing stay unchanged from creation to implementation, anyway.

So, I went back to Hall and told him I'd changed my mind. Not only did I think we could get a golf course in there, but we actually could do two. He said he only wanted one. "In that case," I told him, "we'll give you one really good one."

Over the next few weeks we did our final routing. We cut center lines (lines down the center of a hole that show very roughly the line of play from tee to landing area to green; see page 225). We were making nice progress, and so I made a site visit that I'll never forget. I walked the center lines of the front nine tee-to-green, tee-to-green, and started scratching my head. I didn't really like some of the things I saw, so I turned

An old logging road at Shoal Creek Golf Club, Shoal Creek, Alabama. This is what the site looked like on my first visit in 1974.

around and said, "I'm going to start walking this way for a while." The guys all said, "What are you doing?" I said, "I'm just thinking."

I started walking the other way, green-to-tee. It just started to feel better to me. After a few minutes I said, "Guys, we're going to take this nine the other way." On the spot, we reversed the front nine so that what was originally a green would now be a tee and so on. Hall Thompson will never forget that and neither will I.

The elements that went into that decision show just how much designing and building a golf course really is like assembling a puzzle. The key to the whole thing was the original plan's 3rd hole. The original 9th (current 1st) was all right. The original 8th,

*Hole 6, par-5. This 535-
yard par-5 is a classically
simple risk-reward design.*

a par-3, was all right. No. 7 was a par-4 and started to take you back into a hillside, and there was a creek down there that you couldn't see really well. The next hole, now the 6th, would have been the 4th hole going the other way, and it just didn't sit right with me, and then the next hole, the par-3 going back up into the hill, didn't sit right with me either. We didn't have a really good green site for the next hole. No. 3 was down the hill, which didn't bother me. And the second hole was the 8th that dog-legged back into the hill.

It just seemed to me that I could play a nice hole where No. 1 was, but in reverse. Play off the hill on No. 2. The trouble was the hill. The par-5 3rd hole was the key, because it was a gentle enough slope so that it could get me up the hill.

One of my favorite holes on the golf course is No. 6. It's a 535-yard par-5 in which a creek bed crosses in front of the tee and goes all along the right side of the hole. From the tee you drive over the creek, biting off as much as you want. Then you are faced with an important choice for your second shot. You can either lay up left and play a chip-shot third over water to a bunkered green, or you can go right and go for the green in two, playing over the creek and through a narrow opening between bunkers at the front of the green. It's a wonderful strategy and a classically simple risk-reward decision.

Shoal Creek was full of lessons. There was the importance of thinking freely and creatively. There was the importance of flexibility. And there was the importance of a good owner who could go with change. I can have all the good ideas in the world, but they're useless unless my client goes along with them.

Australian Golf Club

I played in the Australian Open several times in the 1960s and 1970s. I won the golf tournament in 1964, '68, '71, '75, '76, and '78. The last three of those were played at the Australian Club in Kensington, outside Sydney. Over the course of those visits I got to know Kerry Packer, who is one of Australia's most successful businessmen and an ardent sportsman. He approached me after I won in 1976 and said that the tournament organizers had decided to stage the tournament there on a permanent basis. He said he wanted me to redesign the golf course and that he'd "take care of it" (which he did). He was terrific. I remember that we actually worked on the golf course plans while we were fishing the Great Barrier Reef.

The AGC is one of Australia's older courses. Alister Mackenzie did the original 27-hole layout in 1926. I liked his design, but it just didn't have enough fire in it to host a serious national championship every year. With Kerry's blessing, we essentially started over. We put in a new routing. In addition to reversing the nines (the front is

now the back and vice versa) to better accommodate the gallery, we added some water hazards to the golf course, which the original design didn't really have. But the notable thing we did was to create some pretty strong what I call give-and-take holes.

The prevailing wind in Australia is northerly. When they get a storm, the wind shifts to very strong southerly. That happens quite a bit, particularly during their spring, which is when they play the Australian Open (November). These shifts result in very heavy winds. It got so bad that on the 9th hole (which used to be the 18th), you'd play it in the morning and it would be a 3-iron and a sand wedge. In the afternoon, if the southerly kicked up, it could be a driver and a 2-iron. The wind became such a factor that a lot of what I did there was put in side-by-side holes in opposite directions, knowing that one of them would be strong and one weak, depending on the wind. I did that on 7, 8, and 9, and I did it on 16 and 17 as well.

Above: An aerial view of the Australian Club, Kensington, Australia.

Opposite: Australian Club, Kensington. Hole 16, par-4.

Both the 16th and 17th are very long par-4s going in opposite directions. The 16th is a slight dogleg right, about 440 yards, heavily bunkered. The 17th plays through the trees off the tee.

The club had a par-3 golf course they'd play in the morning called the Inner Course. The other one, the 18-hole course, was the Outer Course. I needed more land to design the course Packer had asked for and include a driving range. So I eliminated the Inner Course (I'm sure there are a few members who haven't forgiven me for that yet). It's a pretty darn good golf course, one I'm proud of, and I think it's generally considered one of the best in Australia. Packer wanted a strong, tough golf course and he got it.

Desert Mountain

Desert Mountain in Arizona had its real beginnings in Desert Highlands, the first golf course I did for Lyle Anderson. When I met Lyle in 1980, he told me he wanted a course out in the desert. He had the property already and wanted us to work it. The result was Desert Highlands, my first desert design. We played the first two Skins Games there and the interest in those early Skins Games, combined with the uniqueness of the desert backdrop, drove a lot of interest in golf course development in the desert southwest. Several times I've seen Lyle described in print as the father of desert golf, and considering what he's done for the sport, particularly in Arizona, the description is apt.

Jay Morrish, who was working with me at the time, checked out the site that Lyle had in mind. Jay took one look at the property and nearby Pinnacle Peak and fell in love with the possibilities. I was playing in the Byron Nelson Classic in Dallas, and the next night Lyle came down to Dallas and we met in my hotel room and started working out the concept.

Working in the desert is very delicate. We kept all the grass and all the desert in separate sections and linked them via "transition areas"—waste areas made of dirt and sand. It's since been described as target golf, but what it really is is a way of building a golf course in the desert without using too much water.

At the same time that I was designing Desert Highlands, I was also designing the Country Club of the Rockies in Edwards, Colorado. Both owners said to me, "Jack, we love your golf courses, but your greens are too easy." That's when and why I started putting movement in a lot of my greens. It explains why the greens are so difficult at Desert Highlands and at Country Club of the Rockies. They're really tough.

From Desert Highlands, which was a huge success, I moved along with Lyle to Desert Mountain. What a lot of people don't know is that Pete Dye and his brothers had quite a bit of property in Carefree, Arizona, including what is now Desert Mountain. Roy Dye had actually started a golf course on it. Lyle went up and bought that property for Desert Mountain, and the first course we did was Renegade, where we executed Lyle's idea of having dual greens.

Renegade was supposed to be both the hardest and the easiest of the Desert Mountain courses because of its dual greens. The idea here was that much like offering multiple tees, we'd offer multiple greens. Then we did a sporty course, Cochise, that

Desert Mountain, Carefree, Arizona, Geronimo Course. Hole 18, par-3. Geronimo was originally intended to attract professional tournament play, but the Cochise Course, which hosted The Tradition for many years, turned out to be much more suitable.

Overleaf pages 162 and 163: Renegade Course, hole 12, par-3. Renegade was the first of five courses that I eventually designed at Desert Mountain. Its dual-pin greens were and still are unique.

Overleaf pages 164 and 165: Chiricahua Course, hole 7, par-4. Like all the holes on the golf course, the 7th was built on very severe terrain.

ironically turned out to be the Tradition Course. Then we did Geronimo, which was supposed to be the big, strong course. In fact, if Desert Mountain ever hosted a regular professional tournament, that's where we would have expected it to be played, but Cochise turned out to be a much better course for the gallery. Then we did Apache, which is a really powerful golf course. Of all the Desert Mountain courses, this is the one for which we moved the least dirt. It flows beautifully with the land. Then we did Chiracahua, another big, bold golf course with very severe terrain that dictated even more of a target-golf mentality.

If you like the challenge of designing golf courses, then you'll love the challenge of designing desert golf courses. For one thing, you have the fact that the ball is going to fly a little farther in the desert, and it's going to run a little farther, too. You've got a lot of washes (natural gullies that supply drainage) as opposed to the brooks or creeks you find in parkland golf courses. You play out of the washes, so they're half hazard and half desert.

What I learned about the desert while designing golf courses for Lyle is just how resilient the topography is. We have been very careful to preserve natural environments wherever we work. In the desert, you have to be particularly tender with indigenous plants and animal life. If you do work carefully, you can take an area of the desert, reshape it and revegetate it, and in six months it will look as if it had never been touched. We moved a lot of earth out there. We took entire hills out of the way and did what we had to do, then put them back, and no one who visits the golf course would ever know the difference.

We've done a lot of interesting holes at Desert Mountain. Because they're on television every year, the best-known holes are on the Cochise Course. I've always enjoyed the option-filled 15th hole, which shares an island green with the 7th hole. It's a 548-yard par-5 that tempts the long hitter to reach the well-protected green in two. No. 16 is a bit of a sleeper. It's not an excessively long par-4 at 413 yards, but it plays tough. In the entire history of the Tradition, the field has never averaged par or better here.

Still, the best-known hole at Desert Mountain is probably No. 18 at Cochise. No. 18 is a very reachable par-5, in fact, it really plays like a par-4. 5. You really should make 4 there most of the time, but if you screw up, you can make 5 or 6 pretty quick. Most

of the risk lies in the approach shot. There's very little trouble off the tee, but should you try to reach the green in two, you run the risk of catching the wash that runs in front of the green. Or, if you go long on your second, you can easily end up in a deep rear bunker that plays to a significantly downhill green. Every year at the Tradition, I see at least one guy go for the green and land in either the bunker or the wash and end up playing ping-pong, going back and forth at least once from the bunker to the wash or vice versa. No. 18 has seen its share of drama. It has settled several playoffs and is significant for me as the location of my 100th professional victory (the 1996 Tradition).

English Turn

English Turn is an interesting story. We were looking for a site where we could have a real-estate development as well as a new home for the New Orleans PGA Tour stop. Rather than going out of town and buying high ground, we stayed essentially in town, in New Orleans, and built the course on land that was nine feet below sea level. In fact, the Mississippi River ran right by the mucky property and the river actually stood above the site.

Because the site was only 15 minutes from downtown and right in the middle of everything, it seemed like a good trade-off. It ended up being a handful. It cost $11 million just to get the land up to a level where you could even think about playing golf. Then it cost about $5 million more to build the golf course. Even with all that, it ended up being a great deal. The cost of land outside the city was about $25,000 an acre. It was $10,000 an acre in Algiers. Once we built the ground up we had a great location, and we'd created something accessible to lots of people in the city.

What we had to do first was to provide the drainage and percolation. On a site like that, we use a technique called sand-capping or plating. That's the first golf course I ever used it on. Plating is a way to assist in drainage and provide a good medium on which to grow grass. Basically, you cover a low-lying golf course, or at least the sections saddled with poor soil conditions, with a layer of sand. Water that would ordinarily get trapped between the grass and the perpetually saturated muck underneath it can now trickle through the sand and away from the grass—so you can play on a dry surface. It is somewhat like constructing a putting green (but throughout the golf course), where you have layers of sand, etc., below the surface to assist in drainage. It costs about $1 million to plate a golf course, but in certain regions it's a no-brainer economic decision. A course in heavy-soiled land will pay for its plating very quickly by preventing rain-outs and flooding.

Because the muck couldn't support heavy equipment, we built the course with a dragline. We took the dragline, flipped the dirt over onto the ground, and put wooden pads out. Then we ran our draglines out on them. We knew the dirt would never dry, so we just plopped it in areas. We created our mounds with the draglines, too. We left holes in the designated green areas and in the bunker areas. Once we got the dirt in place with the dragline, we went into the Mississippi and pumped sand out of the river.

We put herringbone drainage throughout the golf course, then put two feet of Mississippi River sand on the golf course. We put extra sand in areas where we planned greens and tees and bunkers, so we could move it around and shape it.

We knew all this dirt would settle, so when we built mounds at English Turn, we built them extra-high. For instance, when the mounds on No. 7 went in, they were approximately 21 feet high. Today, they're about 6 feet high. That's 15 feet of settling in 13 years. We had greens that were built with bulkheads and deadmen (cement anchors that are used to tie bulkheads). After two or three years of settling, the outlines of the deadmen could be seen through the putting surface. One thing did not happen here that we thought would: We created severe undulations in the greens because we expected the settling to flatten the undulations over time. This had actually happened to a lot of greens in the Louisiana Low Country, but because we built those greens very well, and essentially placed them in sand bowls, the greens settled but not like the rest of the golf course. They settled without changing contour. We actually had to go back in a few years later and soften the undulations.

It was a very interesting project, but I'm most satisfied by the fact that if you play this golf course after it rains, it's dry as a bone. For a course below sea level, that is very impressive. It's the best-drained course I know, and a lot of the credit goes to USF&G, who was the financial partner on that project and had the foresight to spend the money and do it right.

Castle Pines

Jack Vickers knew what he wanted: a great golf course in the Denver area that could attract a PGA Tour event. His course opened in 1981, and has hosted the International, the PGA Tour's unique Stableford event, every year since 1986. In Castle Pines he got a beauty. It's a stunning golf course that runs through very rocky mountain terrain. Beautiful ponderosa pines adorn the entire site.

After the beauty of the property, I think of two things when I think of Castle Pines: very rocky ground and high altitude. Castle Pines is the first project I ever designed in truly mountainous topography. I've done quite a few since, and all of them have benefited from the lessons I learned in Colorado. The first lesson was the value—really the necessity—of a southern exposure. When you're building a golf course in the northern climes of the Northern Hemisphere, you will have an easier time growing grass if you give it maximum exposure to the sun. The visual beauty of Castle Pines lies in its mountain setting, but the key to its success is that the entire golf course is built on a south-facing slope.

The next lesson was distance. I'd played plenty of mountain golf, so I was aware of the effect thin air can have on a flying golf ball. I knew that Denver, at a mile high, added about 10 percent to ball flight. With Castle Pines being a little higher up at 6,300 feet, I figured the effect at about 12 percent. This figures to be about 2 percent per 1,000 feet. But this was the first time that I had had to plan for the effects of altitude on every shot of a golf course's strategy.

The third lesson I learned at Castle Pines was the value of a knowledgeable and interested owner. Every time that I've worked with involved, attentive, demanding owners I've ended up with better golf courses. Lyle Anderson and Hall Thompson are excellent examples. Jack Vickers was the same way. Jack wanted one thing: excellence. He is a complete perfectionist, and he really knows and really loves golf.

As beautiful and serene a course as Castle Pines is today, you can only imagine how difficult a piece of property it was to work with. We were faced with this enormous hill, and these ravines—erosion ditches—that ran down a hill covered with staggeringly tall pines. So we had to figure out how to work down through that to the valleys and the washes (the lows), and then, of course, we had to work our way back up the hill to the highs.

Castle Pines Golf Club, Castle Rock, Colorado. Hole 15, par-4. This fairly short par-4 (403 yards) is reminiscent of the 14th at Muirfield Village.

Overleaf: Hole 12, par-4. The area surrounding this pretty hole was originally thickly covered with ponderosa pines.

I originally had the clubhouse positioned farther down the hill, so that you wouldn't play so many holes in a row down or up the hill. My original design had No. 1 and No. 10 going up the hill, but Jack wanted the clubhouse at a higher elevation, so that you could see Pikes Peak from the clubhouse. One of the trade-offs to placing the clubhouse in its current position is that there wasn't much room left near it for a first-rate practice range. The one they have there today is a little too short and you have to hit uphill into the side of the mountain. But that said, Jack was right: His clubhouse does have one of the truly great views in all of golf.

We moved a lot of the ponderosa pines you see on that golf course. I'm talking about huge trees, 30-inch bases and more. We moved and replanted them into strategic locations where you see them today. We also incorporated a lot of the deep erosion arroyos that ran through the property into the design of the golf course, along the 2nd, 3rd, and 4th holes, for example.

A few holes really stand out in my mind. The 3rd is very strong, both aesthetically and strategically. It sits on a piece of the property that was and is wide open, basically free of trees. It's a par-4 with an optional tee shot. It's about a 240-yard carry from the tee to an arroyo that runs into the fairway and then straight down the fairway to the left side of the green. If the wind is at your back, you can go ahead and take it over the arroyo on the right and you'll have a good angle into the green. If you don't want to gamble with the hazard, you can play out to the left on your tee shot, but you're still forced to play over the arroyo on your approach shot. It's a very, very nice hole with clearly delineated options and obvious risks/rewards.

The 12th at Castle Pines is a beautiful little hole. This is one of the areas on the property where we moved a lot of ponderosas. It's got a creek along the left side and a long, narrow green that Jack Vickers enhanced with a beautiful rock outcropping. The 15th is a short par-4 reminiscent of the 14th at Muirfield Village. A shortish tee-shot, probably a 3-wood, followed by a 9-iron or a wedge to a long, thin green that slopes from back to front and is guarded by a lake. If you hit it over the green, you end up in a bunker and are forced to play to a green that's running away from you.

Valhalla

Dwight Gahm and his sons came to me in the early 1980s and said they wanted a golf course outside Louisville, Kentucky, that could host the PGA Championship. Talk about knowing early on exactly what your client wants.

Dwight asked, "What do you think my chances are of getting it?"

I said, "Well, Louisville is a market that the PGA Tour doesn't currently visit. And it's certainly got a decent population base, so I think your chances are very good."

So we did the golf course. It's a nice piece of property that has two really different topographies. The front nine is largely in the flood plain of Floyd's Fork, a river that circles through the golf course. On the front nine in particular, I had to allow for the perpetual swelling and receding of the river while keeping the playing area of the golf course dry. There is also a rock shelf that runs underneath the surface throughout part of the front nine that keeps the water from penetrating the soil and dissipating. If you play Valhalla or see it on television, you'll note that we have a lot of very high elevated tees and greens. That's why—in order to keep them out of the flood plain.

After the linksy, lowland feel of the front nine, the back nine essentially plays through the trees. It's more parkland in its feel. Not that there's a drastic difference in the elevation of the two nines—maybe 50 to 60 feet tops—it's just that one is largely down in the flood plain and the other appears high and dry—although some parts of the back nine, particularly Nos. 13, 15, and 16 are in a flood plain, too.

Well, the Gahms certainly achieved their goal of hosting the PGA Championship. They hosted it in 1996 and again in 2000, my last appearance in the event. They have a Senior PGA Championship slated for spring 2004 and a Ryder Cup scheduled for 2008.

It may have been a little unfair for people to compare Valhalla to its fellow 2000 major championship venues: Augusta National, Pebble Beach, and St. Andrews. It's as good as they come in terms of shot values, but Valhalla was only opened for play in 1986, so it lacks the decades (in the case of St. Andrews, centuries) of history and tradition. In my opinion, Valhalla can stand shot-for-shot with any one of the three. It may even be better, shot for shot. It just doesn't have the history. But when you look at how the majors it has hosted turned out—two playoffs, including the Tiger Woods/Bob May thriller in 2000—and when you look at the coming schedule, it's clear to me that Vahalla is destined for lasting greatness.

Valhalla Golf Club, Louisville, Kentucky. Hole 7, par-5. This hole was designed as a risk-reward gem. However, it has not always been set up that way.

Because there are so many good golf holes at Valhalla, it's hard to single one out, but I think the 7th is very representative of the golf course. The 7th is a 600-yard (from the tips) par-5 dogleg left with a double fairway. It's one of my favorite risk/reward holes anywhere. If you play to the left fairway, which is essentially an island, and you land safely, you have a shorter and relatively simple approach to the green. The problem is that if you miss that fairway, you're either in a hazard or at the very best you're in deep rough. You can kiss birdie and probably par goodbye. But if you can hit the island fairway, the green opens up very nicely from the left.

The other option is to play it down the right fairway. It's a definite three-shot hole from there, but it's a better percentage play for most golfers. You just play your tee ball out to the right, you keep your second down the right side, and you may have a little tougher angle into the green. It's a darn good hole, full of options.

If you ever want to see how much value real risk/reward adds to a hole, compare the way the hole was set up for the 1996 PGA Championship with the way it was set up for the 2000 tournament. Some of you may remember that in 1996 the PGA of America took the left fairway, the island fairway, completely out of play. It was declared out-of-bounds, and if I'm not mistaken, they put a concession stand in there. Played that way, a terrific hole quickly became a boring hole: There were no options. For the 2000 Championship, they set it up the way it was designed to be played, and I think the players really enjoyed it. I know I did.

That was a roller-coaster week for me on several levels. My mother, Helen Nicklaus, died early in the week, so it was a very emotional week from that standpoint. As my mother's health began to decline we discussed this scenario, and she was very insistent that I not withdraw from a tournament to mourn her death. So I played.

On the positive side, I really enjoyed watching and playing with Tiger in the first two two rounds that year. On the negative side, I found out that weekend that I really couldn't compete with PGA Tour fields anymore. Yes, I hit a nice shot into the green at the 36th hole, and only missed the cut by a shot, but I didn't really *compete.*

The emotional icing on the cake at that 2000 PGA was wrapping up the last of my four-major seasons on one of my own designs. Actually, that was the culmination of a theme that ran throughout the year: Three of the four golf courses we played on that year I had either done some work on or designed: Augusta, Pebble Beach, and Valhalla. The only one of the four I've never worked on is St. Andrews.

5 The Elements of Design

One can view golf course design as a giant jigsaw puzzle. The individual pieces are tees and fairways and greens and bunkers and water hazards. And although every course is different, and the thinking behind each of these pieces has to meld in the finished design strategy, I do have some strong feelings about what should or shouldn't go into each of these elements.

It goes without saying that no two golf course projects are identical. You can imagine all the differences not only in what the developer may want, but also in the land and the environment. That said, if my current design work has any hallmarks, I would say they are visibility and containment. By visibility I mean: Try to let the golfer see the hole. Show him where he should be going and show him the trouble that's out there. By containment I mean: Use design to encourage keeping the ball in play. A good example is putting concave slopes in the sides of a fairway to keep decent shots in, or putting a bunker beside or behind the green, not as a penalty but to keep the ball from getting into worse trouble—like woods or water.

*Augusta National Golf
Club, Augusta, Georgia.
Hole 13, par-5. Here is a
great example of a hole
that turns from right to left.*

We look for concave landing areas as opposed to convex ones. That means we're trying to set the holes down in valleys. We're trying to play into contours in a way—keeping the natural lows on the inside of a dogleg where possible. Because it's more enjoyable for the majority of golfers, we prefer to design downhill shots rather than uphill shots, although I will occasionally be forced to go uphill—if you play down, you have to come back up.

I typically like my courses to play from highs to lows. In other words, more often than not I want players to hit from high land over a low to another high piece of land, usually a fairway or a green. I call it slope to counterslope. By hitting from highs to lows or highs to lesser highs, you give the golfer a clear view not only of what's demanded of him, but of the risks and penalties that lie ahead. In designing over 3,600 golf holes in my career, I've done very few blind hazards.

Tees

Tees are probably the most basic, utilitarian element of a golf hole. Simply put, they're just flat areas fitting into landforms. We don't put a lot of emphasis on our tees—we just want them to be flat. We don't aim tees, we don't make square tees, we just try to make free-form platforms that tie naturally into the terrain.

Even though a tee is very simple, clients do spend 50 cents to $1.50 a square foot building one, so you want to make sure that a large percentage of that surface is usable. You don't want to build a tee out so far to one side that a portion is blocked out by rocks or trees. As for size, you want at least, if possible without forcing it, 9,000 square feet of tee space on a par-3. That may sound big, but par-3 tees take the most punishment of any area on the golf course. Instead of having drivers whooshing above the surface, par-3s endure an endless parade of people hitting irons off a very low tee or even no tee. These tees really take a beating. You may need even more than 9,000 feet if it's a high-traffic facility such as a resort or a public golf course. If it's a private club, you can probably do with less.

We try to use at least 6,000 square feet on par-4s and -5s. And, since there's so little play on back tees, we only need to dedicate about 1,000 square feet to those.

Multiple Tees

My thinking on multiple tees has changed. I used to feel that length was the average golfer's biggest problem, so I would sometimes offer a choice of four, five, even six tees to play from. I did that for a while and it seemed to work, but all of a sudden, the golf ball started going noticeably farther. As a result, we had to start moving the back tees farther back. Eventually, we had to move the other tees back in proportion, and suddenly the back tee, the next tee up, and perhaps even the next tee up became too long for the average golfer.

After a few years of doing that, it occurred to me that people couldn't possibly like sitting in their carts and driving past one tee and another and then another just to get to a tee that they felt they could play. Or, even worse, a player may not want to tee it up four tees from the tips, so he moves back and plays it from a distance he really can't handle. Two things may happen then, and from a designer's standpoint they're both bad. He'll have lousy experience, and/or he'll slow down everybody behind him.

The average golfer today is not much better than he used to be (perhaps a bit worse, given the increasing obsession with distance). So now I put in a back tee. I then try to put in a larger second tee, from which most of the membership will play, and I have a ladies' tee. That's all. There's nothing between the members' tees and the very back tees, and that eliminates the pressure for a golfer to upgrade to a tee that's just too long for him. There are exceptions to my three-tee rule on some really long par-4s, super-long par-3s, and some par-5s. On those, if I think it makes sense, we add a fourth tee between the back and the middle tee.

A great example of my new thinking is The Bear's Club, which is over 7,200 yards from the back tees and 6,500 yards from the members' tees. There is no 6,800-yard golf course in there. I'm doing that more and more, because I want the game to be enjoyable for the average golfer while making it a challenge for the better player. Plus, I can always add a tee or two in between if the membership asks for it.

Although tees are pretty simple, determining length isn't their only function. A tee is an integral part of the strategy of any hole. I personally create specific strategies for back tees, forward tees, and ladies' tees. If you don't, you end up with bunkers and hazards that only relate to one set of tees. I also try, where possible, to make the angles of play

toughest from the back tee, a little easier from the members' tee, and then a little easier yet from the ladies' tee. We try not to line them all up in a row, so that you don't look out over a 100-yard chain of tee boxes. Instead, we'll mix it up a little, place some to left or right of center where possible.

As for tunnels off the tee versus wide swaths, most of my longer holes have pretty wide fairways. I like to feel that most of the time you can stand back there with your driver. I think most people, even those who struggle a little with the driver, like to start a long hole with a long club. I know that I don't like to play a golf course where they take the driver out of my hands and make me hit irons off the tee all day. I don't think hitting a 4-iron off the tee is nearly as much fun as hitting the driver. I don't mind hitting or asking golfers who play my designs to hit the occasional 3-wood, but I much prefer the driver.

From tee to green, I like to give the player some idea of where to go and how much room he has to get there. Sometimes, if you play over a hill and you can't make the line of play to the green visible, you can look at the tree line running alongside the course and know at least roughly where to play it. That's the objection I had to some of the first changes made at Augusta in recent years. Take the 9th hole. You never could see the landing area from the tee, but you used to be able to discern the path of the fairway by looking at the trees alongside it. Then they changed the fairway line but not the trees. I don't think that was fair to members or Tour players. Same at No. 11. You were over a hill off the tee and the fairway and the trees didn't match up. They have since corrected much of that.

Fairways

I've always been in favor of generous fairways, particularly off the tee. Many designers go to 25 or 30 yards for a fairway landing area, but I've always tried to get to about 40 or 45 yards. As I said, I like to let the golfer feel he can go ahead and rip it off the tee. But I do try to make sure that within that wider fairway there are a variety of possible outcomes. In other words, I welcome the long ball but I particularly reward the *accurate* long ball. You have to hit the right part of my fairways if you want the easiest shot into the green.

The Challenge at Manele, Lanai City, Hawaii. Hole 12, par-3. The tee positioning and tee options allow any level of player to enjoy the 12th hole fully. While there are five sets of tees here, I have been designing fewer tee boxes on my newer courses.

Other than that, my fairways are pretty straightforward. I don't really like a lot of ridiculous movement—that is, undulation or slope—in my fairways. I don't want the guy who hits a great tee shot on a long par-4 to be stuck with a lousy downhill lie and 225 yards to the hole. What movement you do see in my fairways has a purpose. The idea is pretty simple: Contain the golf ball. One of the ways you do that is by having a player hit from a slope that runs left to right into a slope that runs from right to left—from slope to counterslope. This does several things: It contains shots as they land in the fairway, it enhances a player's confidence as he sets up for his next shot, and it contains that next shot as well.

Think about it. You're a right-handed player. You're standing in the right-hand side of the fairway and the ball is slightly above your feet. A typical grade is in the single digits, perhaps less than 5 percent, but it's enough to help make sure that a moderate hook or slice doesn't get away from you. Earlier we talked about trying to design par-4s and par-5s that encourage or allow the golfer to hit the driver off the tee. This helps in that regard, too. To see a slope that you can use either as an offensive tool for gaining yardage or as a defensive tool to contain your ball is reassuring. Over the span of 18 holes, that constant reassurance can add to the pleasure of the round.

Now, not every hole I do has that built-in safety net. Some holes just don't need it, or they don't have the topography for it. On other holes, I may be looking to inject some difficulty, so I don't use slopes or I use very subtle ones. But, generally speaking, as much as I try to shy away from having a trademark, this receptiveness—slope to counterslope in the fairways and greens and concave rather than convex forms—is probably as much my trademark as anything.

I'm not trying to suggest that this is a concept I created. It's been in common use for some time. Look at the 13th hole at Augusta National. It is a great example of a hole that turns, in this case from right to left, and the low portion of the hole is on the inside of the dogleg. The view from the tee is encouraging to all players, particularly those who can draw the ball. I use this technique a lot in my own designs. The 14th hole at TPC Michigan is a good example. For years, the course has hosted the Ford Senior Players Championship, and for years I've heard complaints from my fellow players about the difficulty of the 14th hole. It's a dogleg left and the fairway slopes from high on the right side to low on the left side, which is bordered for the entire length of the hole, up to and around the green, by a swamp.

Another example is the 3rd hole at The Bear's Club, one of the strongest holes on that course. From the members' tees it's a 400-yard par-4, with a lake that runs all the way along the left-hand side and a fairway that doglegs all the way around the entire lake. It's one of a handful of holes on that course employing that philosophy.

There are exceptions. I'll put the high on the inside occasionally to force the golfer into a different kind of decision. Either you play over the high or you play around it, and there are risks and rewards to each option. The 10th hole at the TPC of Michigan is a dogleg left with high mounding and bunkers all along the high side. You've got to make up your mind to take a gamble and hit it over the top to a narrow fairway and have a shorter shot into the green, or head around the high by taking the ball up the right side, which is a safer play but leaves you with a longer shot to the green.

The Second Shot

The second shot is the most demanding on the majority of my courses. It not only reveals the player, but in many ways reveals the designer as well. The second shot is where you really get to see how a designer integrates his fairways and greens.

There are many considerations that go into fairway landing area design and fairway-to-green design. There are wind, the length of the hole, what hole came previously, what hole or holes are ahead, etc. But one of the most important factors is nature. Whether it's something as obvious as a tree, a river, a lake, or a gulch, or whether it's something as subtle as the natural flow of the land, I try to include it—to feature it really—in the strategy of the golf hole.

The Bull at Pinehurst Farms in Sheboygan Falls, Wisconsin, is one of my latest designs. The 5th hole there has a pretty neat tee shot, but the second shot is unique. You play semiblind, across a gulch into a green that's in a beautiful, natural "punch bowl" setting. The strategy for that entire hole was dictated by the extraordinary green site. We worked backwards from the green to design the other elements of the hole.

*Right: TPC Michigan,
Dearborn. Hole 14, par-4.
The 455-yard 14th is an
example of keeping the
low to the inside of the
dogleg.*

*Overleaf: The Bear's
Club, Jupiter, Florida.
Hole 3, par-4. This hole
also keeps the low on the
inside. It is one of the
strongest holes on a very
strong course.*

Hazards

A large part of the designer's work is deciding where and how (and where not) to insert his hazards. For example, I don't necessarily care to force the golfer to hit the ball 240 yards. What I like to do is make him decide between the glory of the long ball and the practicality of another alternative. Decisions. One part of forcing the golfer to make a decision is working with the land; the other part is creating man-made hazards such as bunkers, water, plantings, or mounds. It all goes back to the routing. If there's a beautiful natural fairway site that just cries out for a bunker in a certain position, then I'll work harder on that fairway strategy, and that strategy will dictate the green shape and the bunkering. Or there may be a great green site that just calls out for a bunker or certain type of pitch or roll, and I'll do that green first and let the green dictate the form of the fairway.

Bunkers

Bunkers obviously come in many sizes and styles. There are deep pot bunkers, long, flat, shallow bunkers, cape bunkers. Some bunkers have all kinds of grasses and plants surrounding them, some are in the middle of greens, some have greens in the middle. Some

Both pages: The Bull at Pinehurst Farms, Sheboygan Falls, Wisconsin. Two views of hole 5, par-4. The quality of the green site dictated the strategy for this hole.

bunkers have a lot of fingers of grass reaching into the sand. There are a million different looks for a bunker, and the looks of the bunkers are integral to the overall look of a golf course.

Royal County Down in Northern Ireland has the most severe bunkers I've ever seen. Not only are they deep, but they have grass and bushes sticking up three or four feet high all around the lip. As most golf fans know, there are many bunkers throughout Ireland and the U.K. that require you to play sideways or even backwards to get out. Even the back door is no guarantee. Gary Player took three shots to get out of one of those bunkers in 2000. All three shots were played backwards. I might not have believed that was possible if I had not had my own train wreck in the aptly named Hell Bunker on the par-5 14th hole at St. Andrews in 1995. During Wednesday's practice round I actually fell into the gaping hazard and had to be helped out by my son Steve, who was caddying for me. Next day, in the first round, I went for the green on my second shot and ended up in the same bunker. It took me four shots to get out.

Common as they are, bunkers may be among the most misunderstood elements of golf course design. After agronomy, they are probably the element that has most evolved since the beginnings of the game.

Opposite: A deep bunker at Royal County Down, Newcastle, Northern Ireland. Hole 3, par-4.

Above: Royal and Ancient Golf Club of St. Andrews, St. Andrews, Scotland. The Old Course, hole 14, par-5. Hell Bunker is aptly named.

Some form of golf has been played at St. Andrews since the 1100s. Back then, when the game was played on pastures and sheep meadows, bunkers were sandy areas at the bases of hills and swales formed by livestock that flocked to the hills to block out the wind. Today, the most important thing about bunkering is that it serves a specific purpose. I use four basic types of bunkers, and each one has its own purpose and a design that helps it achieve that purpose.

Penal Bunkers

Penal means that the bunker is effectively a punishment or penalty for playing a risky shot and failing to execute. It's the golf course equivalent of a speeding ticket: Get caught and you pay. Penal bunkers can be found in the fairway or around the green.

One of my most memorable lessons in penal bunkering came during the grand opening at Muirfield Village in 1974. Johnny Miller joined me for the inaugural round. We were on the par-5 7th hole, a three-shot hole then for most people. You drive it up the fairway, play a long iron down the fairway, and then pitch the ball over a swale into the green. There's a fairway bunker on the left side of the landing area. Johnny put his tee shot in the bunker. I hit my driver safely and laid up with a 2-iron, thinking Johnny would have to lay up out of the bunker. Well, he pured a 5-wood out of the sand and ended up right next to me.

A light went off in my head that day. If a bunker is intended to be penal, it had better *be* penal, otherwise why bother with it? Almost immediately after that round, I had the bunker lowered by about three feet. You can't get out of it now with much more than a 7-iron.

If you look at bunkering throughout Scotland and Ireland, you'll see that almost all of it is penal. The whole course strategy is based on penal bunkering: You put the ball in the bunker and it'll cost you half to three-quarters of a shot. You may be able to advance it from the bunker, you may not. As I said, you may have to play it backwards. At best, you'll pick up 50 or 60 yards. You're now going to be playing a 5-iron to the green instead of an 8-iron.

Some of my bunkers are a little less penal than others—for a reason. Take a fairway bunker that leaves you with either a shot over water to a green or a pitch-out to the fairway. Instead of making that bunker completely penal, I may shallow it up a little bit

Opposite: The infamous Road Hole bunker, left of the 17th green at St. Andrews, is one of the most challenging penal bunkers in the world.

Overleaf: This greenside bunker, which guards the 9th green at Pebble Beach, is very reminiscent of its U. K. counterpart.

to plant the seed in the golfer's head that he just might be able to get home. That way, I'm encouraging him to make a decision. If he breaks my cardinal rule of golf (never follow a bad shot with a dumb shot) and goes for the carry over water, he'll either be rewarded terrifically or he'll be staring at a double-bogey. If I had made that bunker penal, the golfer would have no decision to make.

Directional Bunkers

If penal bunkers are like speeding tickets, then directional bunkers are like road signs. They actually help a player by directing him. They are very often placed beyond the turning point of a dogleg or on the outside edge of the turn. They are largely out of reach off the tee or easily carried; their only purpose is to aid the golfer in terms of the shape or direction the hole is taking. They also assist in depth perception by showing the width of the fairway. Whereas a penal bunker, with its high lip and deep bottom, is intended to trip a player up, the directional bunker may have a lower lip and shallower bottom.

The 14th hole at English Turn is a 460-yard dogleg left, played over low rough on the left. I did not want to penalize a golfer for taking the long route, so I put in directional bunkers saying, "Okay, hit it over here, but hit it inside this."

Aesthetic Bunkers

The term aesthetic bunker is fairly self-explanatory. These bunkers are there to beautify. They're accessories. The two bunkers at the 3rd hole at Muirfield are aesthetic bunkers and directional as well. They're not even close to being in play, but they lighten up the view. You have a similar bunker on the 10th hole at Augusta. You stand in the fairway and that bunker looks very, very pretty, but it serves no strategic purpose. I mean, how often do you see anyone in it? (Now I'll probably end up in it next year.) You can't drive the ball into it and there's virtually no chance of a professional being in it on his second shot. So its sole purpose is to beautify the hole, and it does a fine job of that.

Functional Bunkers

Although few of the players who get into these bunkers would believe me, functional bunkers are really installed as a service to the golfer. Maybe you're playing to an uphill green and your shot runs off the back of the green and you don't know what's back there. Very often, I'll slip a bunker in there just to contain the ball. That way it may avoid some woods, water, or a worse fate.

The bunker to the left along the 18th at Pebble Beach is a functional bunker. If you snap-hook a ball off the fairway there and it goes out over the ocean, nothing is going to stop it from going in. But if you just hit the ball with a little too much of a draw, you'll land in this bunker and be spared the more severe hazard. That's the function of it.

Same with the 18th hole at English Turn. It's a long hole. I didn't want to kill the golfer by putting the water directly in play, so I put in a functional bunker along the left. If you hit it a little left, you are not completely penalized. The bunker keeps you dry, but leaves you with a hard-enough shot.

Water

Over the years, I've found that you have to be judicious with water hazards. While it's nice to have water on a golf course, too much can present a problem. Not only is there an obvious problem with playability, but water-laden properties present another, subtler problem.

A good example is Great Waters, a course I designed for Reynolds Plantation in Greensboro, Georgia. My biggest problem there was taking enough holes *off* the water on the back nine so that not *all* nine of them would be on Lake Oconee. I tried to achieve a balance between keeping the water in view and keeping the water in play. A stream weaves in and out of the golf course on the front nine holes, but only the 9th green actually brings the lake into play. On the back nine, the lake comes into play on five or six holes. Too much beautiful waterfront land is a wonderful problem to have, but it does complicate the design process.

Look at Pebble Beach. You have one of the greatest stretches of holes anywhere in the world there with Nos. 4, 5, 6, 7, 8, 9, and 10 all on the ocean. What a fabulous

Muirfield Village Golf Club, Dublin, Ohio. Hole 3, par-4 These are aesthetic bunkers.

Overleaf pages 202 and 203: English Turn Golf and Country Club, New Orleans, Louisiana. Hole 18, par-4. This is a functional bunker. It can keep you dry, but it can also leave you with a bear of a shot into the green.

Overleaf pages 204 and 205: Reynolds Plantation, Greensboro, Georgia. Great Waters Course, hole 18, par-5. Lake Oconee provided a gorgeous backdrop for this golf course. The key for me was to use the water views in moderation.

stretch of holes. But can you imagine if the first three and the last eight were also on the water? Suddenly, we wouldn't be talking about a great stretch, we would be talking about a four-hour blur in which all 18 holes blended into one seaside sensation. As neat as that might sound to people who love to play seaside golf, it would take away from the designers' ability to provide the round with rhythm and balance. It would also be hard to make a particular hole stand out from the others. When you finished playing, you wouldn't remember particular holes because they all looked alike. So when you're putting in hazards, man-made or natural, you try to balance them out by putting them in a certain place or in a position in the round where they have some importance.

When we have a piece of property with normal drainage, I try to get water into six or seven holes. By water I mean what we call "nonrecoverable hazards" that are strategically in play. I do occasionally include water for aesthetic reasons. There's a creek that runs down the left side of hole No. 1 at Muirfield, but I took it functionally out of play. You rarely see anybody in there. I could have found a way to bring that creek into play, but decided not to. I left the creek in on hole No. 2, kept it mostly out of the tee shot on the 3rd except that we play across it into a pond. It's out on the 4th. Then I use it strategically on the second half of the 5th hole, and it makes various strategic and aesthetic appearances throughout the remainder of the course. On the 11th, I actually based the hole on the creek. It runs through No. 12 in the form of a lake. It's out on 13, back in play on 14. It's there on 15, but not tight. I could have taken the fairway in tight to it on the tee shot but didn't, and then I brought it in a little on the second. It's out on 16 and 17 and then back in play on 18. The point is that even though the creek runs all through those holes, I picked my spots. Because of that, each of the holes has its own character, with the creek tying them all together thematically. I highlight it in some places and downplay it in others. That's employing balance in the use of nonrecoverable hazards.

Greens

Like bunkers, greens are an element of both strategy and design. They also play a critical role in aesthetics. Greens can be little or tiny, big or huge. They can be middle-size. They can have contours or they can be flat. They can be elevated or depressed, crowned à la Donald Ross, large with sweeping contours, or mid-size with sweeping contours à la Mackenzie. They can be large and flat and deadly dull, which you see in a lot of American golf course designs circa 1960–70. Actually, one of the reasons I got interested in golf course design was the sheer number of bad greens I saw being built in the 1960s.

Like tees, greens don't exist in a vacuum. The green's size, shape, and location are influenced by the rest of the hole according to the hole's shape and length. The expected clientele of the course also dictates certain characteristics. Public courses and resort courses generally require larger greens, because of the heavy player traffic and the way in which it converges at the hole location. These greens would wear out in a matter of weeks unless they were large enough to handle multiple hole locations. But you may not need to build a particularly large green even at a public or resort course if you don't put in too many contours. A small, flat green will supply as many possible hole locations as a large, contoured one.

Take greens like those at St. Andrews, which are among the largest in the world. They're fabulous because of their contours and the elements of strategy on the approach shots, as well as the contours in the greens themselves. Look at the greens at Augusta. They've changed significantly over time. Mackenzie had very severe greens, but as bentgrass and maintenance technologies progressed and allowed putting surfaces to be grown shorter and faster, his contours became too severe and required softening.

Another important aspect of green design is remembering that there is more to a green than the green itself. You often hear designers talk about "the green complex." This is not a psychological condition. The green complex is the entire area around the green—consisting of the green, the slopes around the green, greenside bunkers, and any other hazards or features that may tie directly into the green.

For instance, when I design a green I'm not just thinking about the approach shot and the putt. I'm thinking about the player who misses the green. Where is he likely to miss? What type of shot will he, or should he, be left with? Do I want to encourage a player to play a certain shot?

Aerial view of Pebble Beach Golf Links, Pebble Beach, California. Can a designer be blessed with too many ocean views? I think Pebble Beach does a great job of weaving play to and away from the water.

Overleaf: Royal and Ancient Golf Club of St. Andrews, St. Andrews, Scotland. The greens at holes 11 and 7. St. Andrews putting surfaces are among the largest in the game.

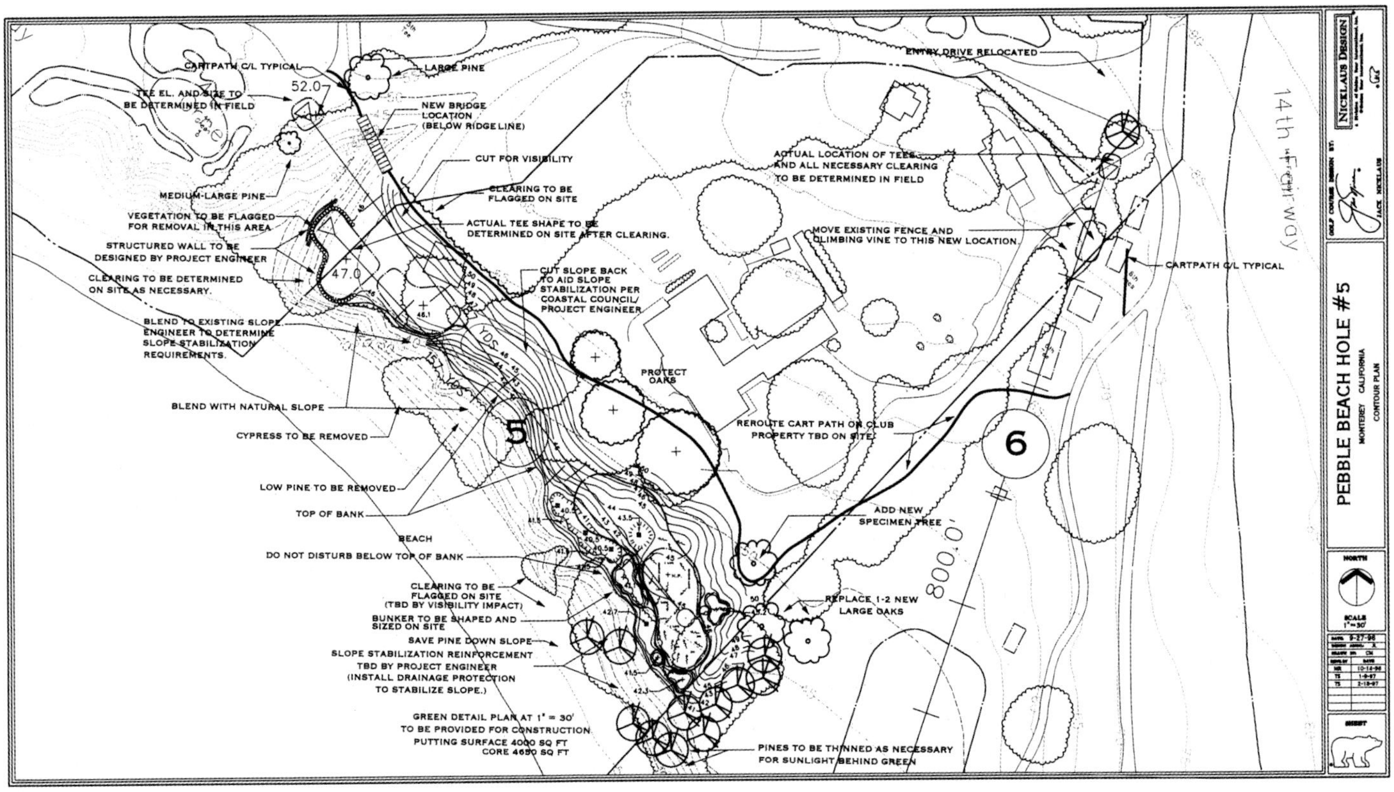

CARTPATH C/L TYPICAL
LARGE PINE
TEE EL. AND SIZE TO BE DETERMINED IN FIELD
52.0
NEW BRIDGE LOCATION (BELOW RIDGELINE)
CUT FOR VISIBILITY
MEDIUM-LARGE PINE
CLEARING TO BE FLAGGED ON SITE
VEGETATION TO BE FLAGGED FOR REMOVAL IN THIS AREA
ACTUAL TEE SHAPE TO BE DETERMINED ON SITE AFTER CLEARING.
STRUCTURED WALL TO BE DESIGNED BY PROJECT ENGINEER
CLEARING TO BE DETERMINED ON SITE AS NECESSARY.
47.0
CUT SLOPE BACK TO AID SLOPE STABILIZATION PER COASTAL COUNCIL/ PROJECT ENGINEER
BLEND TO EXISTING SLOPE. ENGINEER TO DETERMINE SLOPE STABILIZATION REQUIREMENTS.
PROTECT OAKS
BLEND WITH NATURAL SLOPE
5
CYPRESS TO BE REMOVED
LOW PINE TO BE REMOVED
TOP OF BANK
BEACH
DO NOT DISTURB BELOW TOP OF BANK
CLEARING TO BE FLAGGED ON SITE (TBD BY VISIBILITY IMPACT)
BUNKER TO BE SHAPED AND SIZED ON SITE
SAVE PINE DOWN SLOPE
SLOPE STABILIZATION REINFORCEMENT TBD BY PROJECT ENGINEER (INSTALL DRAINAGE PROTECTION TO STABILIZE SLOPE.)
GREEN DETAIL PLAN AT 1" = 30' TO BE PROVIDED FOR CONSTRUCTION
PUTTING SURFACE 4000 SQ FT
CORE 4650 SQ FT
ENTRY DRIVE RELOCATED
14th Fairway
ACTUAL LOCATION OF TEES AND ALL NECESSARY CLEARING TO BE DETERMINED IN FIELD
MOVE EXISTING FENCE AND CLIMBING VINE TO THIS NEW LOCATION.
CARTPATH C/L TYPICAL
REROUTE CART PATH ON CLUB PROPERTY TBD ON SITE.
6
ADD NEW SPECIMEN TREE
800.0'
REPLACE 1-2 NEW LARGE OAKS
PINES TO BE THINNED AS NECESSARY FOR SUNLIGHT BEHIND GREEN
NICKLAUS DESIGN
JACK NICKLAUS
PEBBLE BEACH HOLE #5
MONTEREY CALIFORNIA
CONTOUR PLAN
NORTH
SCALE 1"=30'

Pebble Beach Golf Links, Pebble Beach, California. This was the original drawing of hole 5. As the hole went in, and upon viewing it in the field, I added a bounce-in on the left side which makes the hole play more fairly.

I'll give you an idea of how integral the area around a green is to a well-designed hole. In the 2000 U.S. Open at Pebble Beach, the USGA decided to grow rough in the little fairway patch we put in the front-left of the 5th green. If you look at the blueprint, you can see a slope that runs the length of the left side of the hole. We set the green in the location we did and at the angle we did in order to make the most of that slope in our strategy. The hole plays roughly 187 yards from the back tee. Because it will play into a crosswind more often than not, I thought I'd give the golfer a choice—two ways to play the hole. The obvious way is to fly a 4- or 5-iron right at the pin. Then I offered what I thought was a smarter shot, a percentage shot. You feed the ball off the slope on the left (which tops off at about 50 feet above sea level), and let the ball follow the lay of the land onto the green (the right side of which measures only 42 feet above sea level). Gravity does the rest.

I disagreed with the USGA's decision to grow rough in the bounce-in area not only because it took the option out, but also because it eliminated what I consider to be the *better* option, the smarter play. As a result, this simple par-3 played the hardest of all 18 holes in the Open. Pebble Beach has since adopted the original design, but I think the Open incident shows that good greens are not designed in a vacuum, but are inexorably linked to the land around them.

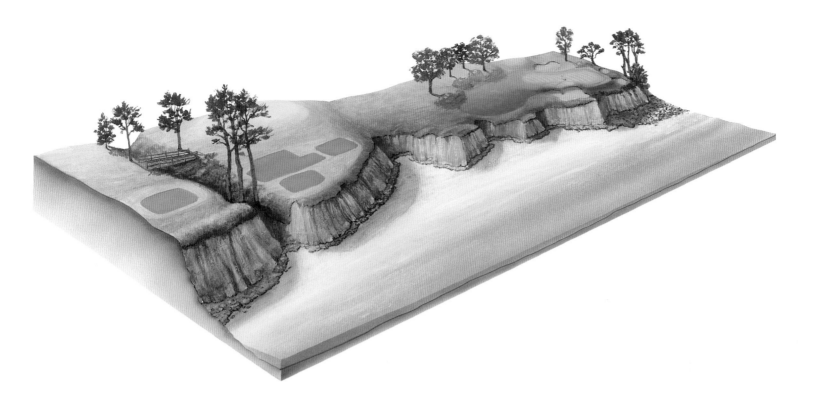

Greens are vitally important. The green is the consummation of the hole. That's why, unlike some designers who are known for a certain type of green, I design all kinds. Greens have to serve so many masters: They have to serve the property, the wishes of the owner, the strategy of the course in general and of that hole in particular. So I'll do small and flat. I'll do medium with a lot of pitch and slope. I'll do middle size with a lot of rolls. I'll do large with big rolls. It all depends on what the situation calls for.

A related aspect of green design is often overlooked, even by experienced designers: Whatever its style, a green must ultimately match the scale of the surrounding property. If you have a big open space out West somewhere with wide, impressive views and sweeping horizons, you have to increase the size of the greens to meet that scale. Tiny little postage stamps don't fit into that kind of setting and end up being overpowered. In situations where that happens, golfers and critics are often unsure of what the disconnect is, but it's usually the discord between the scale of the surroundings and the scale of the design element—specifically, the greens.

The area surrounding the property sometimes dictates the scale of the golf course even more than the property itself does. In other words, I may have 160 acres of land with minimal movement, minimal resources from which to take my design cues, but I may have a mountain range in the distance and that will be the key to my scale for structures such as fairways and greens.

Pebble Beach Golf Links, Pebble Beach, California. Hole 5, par-3. This rendering shows the fairway along the left side of the green, the way the hole was designed to be played.

Overleaf: TPC at Snoqualmie, Washington. Hole 14, par-4. This driveable par-4 is built to match its surroundings.

Grass

Most people, even avid golfers, think that grass is grass. The fact is that grass selection, rather than being a simple choice made at the end of the project, is a vital decision made very early on in the design/construction process. One of the first things we get from a prospective client is the weather data for his property, so that our agronomists can select the grass that best matches the project's weather profile, soils, traffic demands, budget, and playability requirements.

There are two basic types of golf course grasses: warm season and cool season.

WARM SEASON: Bermudas are the grasses most used on warm-season courses. They love hot weather, and won't thrive unless the temperature regularly gets above 80 degrees. It used to be that all you had to work with in warm climates was common Bermuda, which is really too coarse to be optimal for golf. Some courses do use it for roughs, but you won't see it in the fairways anymore.

Then came the hybrid Bermudas (most of these have the familiar "T-I-F"—they were developed in Tifton, Georgia—prefix, such as tifdwarf, tifgreen, tifway. Some also have numerical designations, such as tifton 419). Basically, this family was formed when researchers in pursuit of the ultimate grass gathered samples from different golf courses in different areas, radiated them, and selected the ones with the most promising characteristics.

Some players say that the ball sits up a little better on a Bermuda fairway. That's because each individual blade stands so erect and is so rigid that the ball literally rests on the tips of the blades. When you putt on Bermudagrass, all you really need to know is that the greens tend to grow toward the setting sun. Factor that in when you're reading Bermuda greens and you'll putt much more effectively. Once the green ages and gets a little mottled, the sunset effect may weaken, but it's always there to some degree.

COOL SEASON: Bentgrass is the most-used cool-season grass. It generally grows more laterally than Bermuda.

Unlike Bermudagrass, in which the break of the green is dictated by the setting sun, bentgrass follows the land's natural drainage. When you're putting on a bentgrass green, look around. Try to spot the highs and lows of the green and determine where water would naturally flow off the surface. Factor that into your break and you'll score much better.

Hybrid Bermuda

Poa annua Invading Turf

There are hundreds, perhaps thousands of different species and hybrids of grass. Proper grass selection is critical from the standpoint of maintenance, playability, and aesthetics.

Agrostis stolenifera (Creeping Bentgrass)

Festuca rubra (Chewings Fescue) 'Banner'

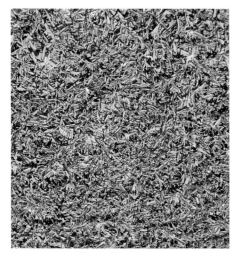

Agrostris spp. 'Bent Grass'

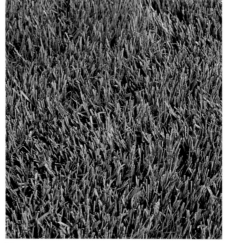

Fescue

Poa pratemsis 'Kentucky Bluegrass'

Zoysia tenuifolia

One of the most dramatic differences in playability between bent and Bermuda arises when chipping into the grain. I don't have all that much trouble chipping on bent, even into the grain, but when I play a chip shot into the grain on Bermudagrass, I'm particularly careful. Bermudagrass has very thick, stubborn blades, and it's easy to stub the leading edge of your club. There's a very delicate balance between stubbing the club and skulling the chip. It takes a great deal of touch and concentration. Bermuda rough is also notoriously tough.

Early on, bentgrass was primarily used for greens, but over the last hundred years it has become sought-after first for tees and then for fairways. That evolution is inextricably linked to modern irrigation.

Manual irrigation of fairways began in the 1940s and early 1950s, and it became automated in the 1960s. That development—the ability to irrigate an entire golf course automatically—is one of the biggest advances in the history of grass and grass maintenance. With the arrival of the computerized irrigation systems, if you wanted to water for three minutes, it watered for three minutes down to the second. Back in the 1950s, you'd plug the sprinkler into a coupler valve in the fairway and the guy would ride a cart around and keep changing these things all night long. With so much human element involved, it was all extremely imprecise. But with the advent of automated irrigation, the better controlled the water was, the more the bentgrass thrived.

Which is which? If you're curious about what type of grass you're playing on, just look at the blades. Close up, a blade of Bermudagrass resembles a tree. Each stem or shoot comes up and has little branches where the leaf points come off at about a 90-degree angle from the stem. If you let Bermuda grow too high, those leaves come up and affect the roll of the ball.

With bentgrass, the leaves come out of the crown of the plant and they're wrapped around and they just keep flowing out from the base. It's a totally different growth mode. Of course, bent and Bermuda are not the only grasses used on golf courses today.

Bluegrass

Bluegrass is very common. It is often used in areas that have severe winter weather—for instance, you'll find it on many golf courses in the Rocky Mountain region. It's not a favorite of mine, because it tends to let the ball sink down too much, but owners often want it because it is very hardy and disease resistant. Some of the new blends of bluegrass are better than they used to be, but from a playability standpoint, I think it is inferior to bentgrass.

Poa annua (Annual Bluegrass)

Po, as it's frequently called, is without doubt the most misunderstood grass in the game. An annual bluegrass, it has a notorious reputation among weekend golfers. It is not uncommon to hear players bemoan the presence of "po" in their greens, yet the truth about *Poa* is that while it does have its minuses, it also has meaningful pluses. From course design, maintenance, and playability standpoints, it seems you can't live with it, and can't live without it.

Poa annua is a winter annual, which means that it germinates in the late summer or fall, lives through the winter, then dies in the spring. Like many grasses, at some point it goes to seed. You see it mostly in the spring, when the seed heads are at their lightest color, and the small light-color "flowers" are visible even at a very low cut.

So if greens are comprised of bent or Bermuda, how does *Poa* get a foothold? Each *Poa annua* plant produces multitudes of seeds, which are then carried throughout the course by various means. We track them on our shoes, on our clubheads, on the tires of our golf carts. If there's any weakness in a green's existing grass, especially an unrepaired ball-mark, the *Poa* will move in and fill the void. The first evidence of *Poa* shows up in your green as very small patches of silvery-white grass.

Although it is considered a weed, other grasses thrive alongside it. That's one of *Poa's* problems. It volunteers itself into a pure bentgrass or Bermuda green, and as the ball tracks across the green, it hits different textures of grass that deflect it, affecting the speed and even the direction of a putt. This inconsistency gets even worse during the seed-head phase, because the seed head grows at twice the rate of the leaf and of the other grass around it. So you get not only inconsistent surfaces, but inconsistent grass heights as well. As a result, putts will be deflected unless the greens are mown two or

219

three times a day—which is highly impractical. Otherwise the inconsistency will only get worse.

Poa is also a negative in that it has very shallow roots, not much of a root system at all, and because it is annual in type. You get a hot day and low humidity and you're not watching it, it's gone.

Since Poa is so susceptible to weather, you will very rarely see it used as a primary grass. But in Poa's defense, if you had 100 percent Poa annua on your greens and you had the ability to properly manage it, you'd have a very nice putting surface. If you look at the golf courses that make up the unofficial rota of U.S. Open venues—Olympic, Baltusrol, Oakmont, Shinnecock, Pebble Beach, or Winged Foot, you will see that they're all primarily Poa annua greens. That's because they don't have a choice, and from a pure putting standpoint, Poa annua is one of the finest surfaces you'll ever find. The only problem is mixing it with other grasses and that two- or three-week period in the spring when it's throwing off seed heads.

Fescue

I try to use fine fescue wherever the climate is right. I like the turf over in the U.K., and most of that is fescue. One of its best features is that it does not require a great deal of water or many chemicals. It takes a little longer than some other grasses to grow in, but once it takes hold, it makes a terrific turf. Among my more recent projects, I used fescue at Old Works in Anaconda. I used it at Roaring Fork in Colorado, too. I probably would have used it in many other places, but clients tend to shy away from it because they don't understand it.

While I will use fescue as a fairway grass, I particularly like it in the rough. I like the spacing between the blades. Unlike bluegrass rough, it is tall and fine and leaves enough space between the blades so that you can swing the golf club through it. From the standpoint of aesthetics, I also like the color, especially the tan color it takes on late in the summer.

Zoysia

Zoysia is another grass we use in the mid-section of the country—Tennessee through Oklahoma. I've probably put zoysia into about a half-dozen courses. Like fescue, it takes a little while to grown in. It makes a nice fairway grass, but I'm not wild about it in the rough. Like fescue or Bermuda, zoysia offers a good, tight knit that allows the ball to sit up nicely, at least in the fairway.

We choose grasses for several reasons. Who is going to play it? What is the developer's budget? What is the pro forma maintenance budget?

Let's say I'm building a golf course in a state park in the Midwest. It's a public golf course, the developer is planning on 50,000 rounds a year, and you have modest development and maintenance budgets.

First, I'll need to create greens and green sizes that will handle traffic. I'll need fairways large enough to withstand a lot of abuse. The tees will have to be big enough that if they get torn up, they'll have time to recover. Then I want the hardiest grass for quick recovery and ease of maintenance, and I want the best quality for the money, the best value. So what grass would I choose? I would probably go with a bluegrass/fescue combination or a bluegrass/bent combination, something that is fairly hardy, that can take wear and tear. And I would probably do the same thing with the tees.

For the greens, I'd probably pick a bentgrass with minimal problems. Consider a course like Muirfield Village or Valhalla, both of which were designed specifically with world-class fields in mind. There you need the best possible putting surface, so you'll go to the highest-tech class that you can. A good analogy is the floor covering in your own home. When it comes to the hallway from the garage into the mudroom, you'll probably want a low maintenance, inexpensive, durable throw rug. You might even drop a remnant out there. But in the living room, your needs and your priorities are different. The traffic is lighter, the wear and tear less brutal, plus you want the best in the room where you entertain company. Any smart homeowner picks furnishings by budget and usage and then gets the best quality for the money. Grassing golf courses is really no different.

6 The Making of a Golf Course

I need to know: Who is my client and what does he want? Are we working on a resort or a private club? Is the owner concerned with selling lots? If it is residential, we create a layout with as much solid golf product as possible. That means we may sacrifice some topographical assets to allow the developer the proper number of lots. If the assignment is strictly core golf, and all they want is the best golf course possible, then we'll take advantage of all the natural characteristics of the land. It starts with the client.

*The Bear's Club,
Jupiter, Florida. Hole
17, par-4. A lot has to
happen before raw land
can be transformed into
a beautiful golf hole
like the 17th at The
Bear's Club.*

Routing

The next step is to provide the client with a basic plan to take to his local government for planning and zoning approvals. This plan will usually include an initial "routing" of the golf course, outlined on a topographical map or "topo."

When you route a golf course, you try to play through the valleys as much as you can, playing from slope to counterslope. You try to build your greens low and your tees high in order to play as close to downhill as possible. Very often in a good routing you end up taking the path of least resistance.

Once we've looked at the site, both in person and through topographical maps, we look at the highs and lows on paper and sketch out the path of the golf holes, the path that best utilizes the land and encourages good holes. We spend a lot of time on this paper stage because we can make changes very cheaply with an eraser. Changes cost our clients a lot more when they're made with a bulldozer. We outline each hole and where it would fall on the land. These early routings include no strategy (details on exactly how the hole would play). In other words, we may show that we plan to use a stretch of land along a lake, but we probably won't decide for some time whether that hole will be a par-4 or a par-5.

Then we go out and stake the routing. That means going to the site and literally putting stakes in the ground to represent the centers of tees, landing areas, and greens. The imaginary line these stakes create is called the hole's "center line." With minimal clearing to this point, the center line gives us a way to walk the property as a potential golf course and to see whether the proposed routing works.

From that point we may not see the client for anywhere from a few months to a few years—it is not unusual for a developer to spend that much time getting his approvals. Some potential clients never do get them and those projects die on the vine.

I'm involved early on in looking at topos of the property and perhaps making a preliminary site visit. I usually get in on the original routing, too, because sometimes, depending on a client's approval process, the original routing may not be changeable. But I don't get too deeply involved again until we are sure we can actually build a golf course and all the access roads and water supply/drainage that we'll need.

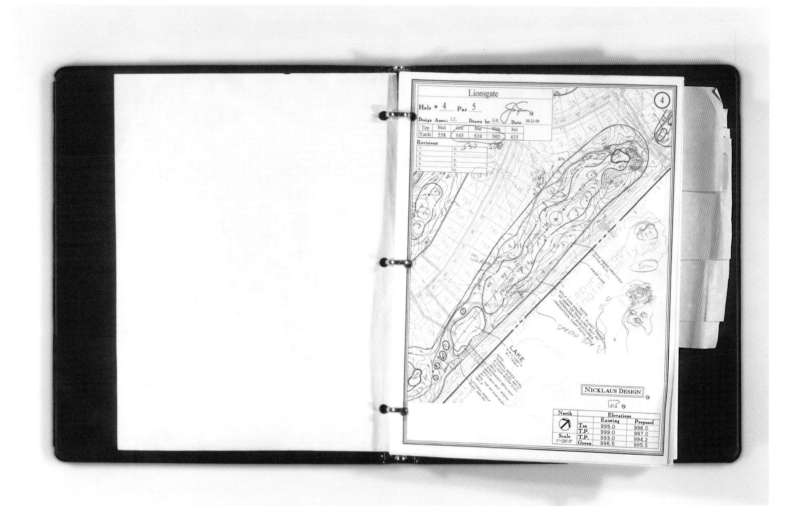

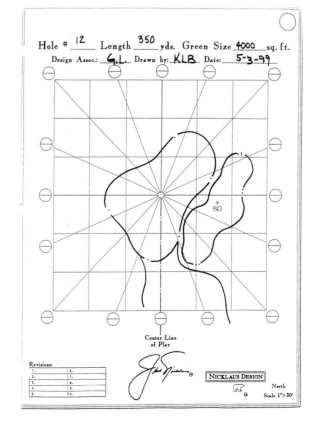

Above: A field sketchbook.

Left: The center line is clearly shown in this early design for the green complex at the 12th hole at The Bear's Club. It was ultimately discarded, but was used as a starting point.

Routing map superimposed on a topographical map. Grand Bear (earlier named Grand Pines) is a great example of how a good routing tries to follow the path of least resistance.

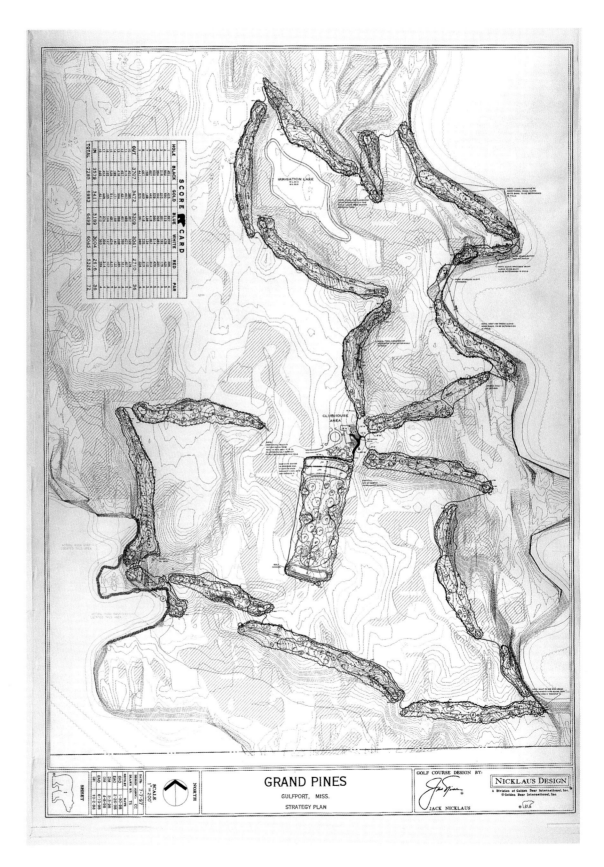

Once we get close to beginning construction of the golf course, we start working with the owner to nail down a final plan and specific costs.

Next, clearing begins from the center line out. That is, we start by moving laterally from the center line out toward the rough. This is intentionally a slow process. If we were to just rip through the landscape from center line to the edges of the playing area, we would run several risks. First, we might end up clearing several acres of property only to realize that the hole cannot be built there. If that happens, there's no going back. Second, we might inadvertently destroy the kind of unique characteristics that often give golf holes their personality. It is not at all uncommon to find a handsome rock out-

Grand Bear, Saucier,
Mississippi. Hole 17,
par-4.

cropping or stand of trees that were not well represented on the maps and the initial site visits. It happens all the time. Sometimes I'm forced to take them out, sometimes I'll not only keep them but I'll use them to accent the hole. Sometimes we have to adjust the land plan to do it. The Loxahatchee Club in Jupiter, Florida, is a good example.

The land plan for Loxahatchee didn't show much in the way of dramatic vegetation, just a lot of trees and bushes. We went ahead and cut the lakes. The 11th was originally a par-3 that was supposed to play out to a point on one of the lakes, but from the 11th green all the way to the 12th green we found the nicest pine forest on the entire property. So I redesigned the 11th hole into a short par-4 (infamous for its humps in the fairway), and then jumped around the forest to play No. 12, a par-3, alongside these beautiful trees. That's an example of where we got too far down the road in clearing and construction before we realized what we had. We made a mistake, but were able to turn it into a positive.

Right: The Bear's Club, Jupiter, Florida. Hole 18, par-5. This hole was revised to keep the setting sun out of the members' eyes. Now it's a great reachable par-5.

If anyone ever claims that he doesn't make mistakes in designing or building golf courses, he's lying. You just have to approach it as you would a mistake during a round: Get out of trouble without multiplying your problems. I had a similar experience with the last few holes at The Bear's Club. We failed to realize that, as originally designed, the 17th hole and the 18th hole would have played into the setting sun in the spring-time, which I did not want my two finishing holes to do. It can be beautiful, but it can also pose maddening visibility problems. How could we not have noticed this detail? We did most of the design work in the fall, when the sun was in a different position. I solved the problem by shortening the 15th hole, originally a par-5, into a par-4. Then I inserted the 16th hole as a par three. I made the 17th a par-4 and the 18th, which was originally a par-3/4, became a par-4/5. The tee shot on the 18th hole still plays into the sun, but by lengthening the hole I was able to add a change of direction and for the most part take the sun out of the members' eyes.

At Muirfield Village we had a unique problem, not so much with nature as with borders. A lot of people don't know that Muirfield Village Golf Club is situated in two Ohio counties. The Delaware County–Franklin County line actually runs right through the practice putting green. So, given that we wanted a full-service clubhouse and that Delaware County is a dry county and Franklin is wet, we had a hard time sit-ing the clubhouse. The place we were left with to build the clubhouse was essentially a 30-foot-deep hollow just inside the Franklin County line. The clubhouse is built on about 30 feet of fill. Now the placement of the clubhouse was going to affect the place-ment of the 18th green, so before we built the building we went up in a cherry-picker to scout the location for the green. Right in front of where we wanted to put it there was a huge hickory tree, and I didn't have the heart to tear it down. But by putting the clubhouse where we did, I had to move the green back about 30 yards, which put the tree in the way. I remember the day I finally made the decision about the tree. I tried to find a way to save it and play around it, but eventually realized it had to go. As soon as I said the words, my men whistled to a guy on a bulldozer who was hiding behind a stand of trees. In less than 10 seconds he hit the tree and took it down. If you look at the 18th hole at Muirfield Village today, there's a little ridge 20-25 yards short of the green. That was the original green site and that's just about where this tree stood. From that portion of the 18th all the way up to the clubhouse is fill.

I don't even begin to think about the strategy of the golf course or of the individual holes until these corridors are opened, because I don't want to get ahead of the project and end up trying to fit the round peg of my strategy into the square hole of the corridor. I like to *see* the golf course evolve, not plan it in the office. First of all, it's more fun that way. Second, you always end up with a better course. In recent years, people have been talking about computer-assisted design (CAD), and we have excellent CAD capabilities in our offices, but no computer is going to out-design a well-trained, deeply experienced human mind. Computers can give us a lot of valuable information, but they still can't imagine.

Then we'll walk the site. The light clearing gives us a sneak preview of the way the hole may look or play when finished. We'll see better how the holes will lie in there and make adjustments accordingly. Even with all the work we do on paper there's no substitute for being there. Maybe as important as anything on the map is what you might find off it. We can lay out an initial routing on paper that seems perfect, and then get to the site and realize there's a stunning mountain range ten miles outside the site that wasn't included on the map. Sometimes those changes are made very early in the initial routing stages, but I've made some pretty drastic ones in midstream. I did a golf course in Lake of the Ozarks called The Club at Porto Cima where I reversed the entire front nine. The 9th green became the first tee and off we went. As I mentioned earlier, we did the same thing at Shoal Creek. It made sense. Recently, I visited a project out in the Midwest and pretty much reversed the front nine there. In that case, there was one stubbornly awkward hole. To get that hole to work, I took a look at going the other way. When I studied how that would affect the other holes, I realized that it actually made them better. That particular developer was very focused on selling real estate, and in the beginning the change made him understandably nervous, because he didn't want to depart from his well-thought-out real-estate plan. But it turned out that when we reversed the nine, he actually picked up lots. Very often golf course design, even among the most respected names in the business, is a think-on-your-feet exercise.

Overleaf pages 234 and 235: The Bear's Club, Jupiter, Florida. Hole 16, par-3. The 16th was born when I rearranged 17 and 18.

Overleaf pages 236 and 237: The Summit Course at Cordillera, Edwards, Colorado. Hole 16, par-3. The theme and scale for this Rocky Mountain course matches the theme and scale of the surroundings.

Now we start to generate a "theme" and a "scale" for the golf course. Suppose we are in Mississippi: gently rolling hills, tall pine trees, sand underneath. We could do a variety of things architecturally. We could do an Augusta National–type pristine parkland look; a Pinehurst No. 2 look where it's all jagged edges, sandy with Bermuda creeping out. Maybe there's nothing on site, no character. Maybe there's no water table. In that case, maybe we'd consider a more linksy look.

It all gets back to for whom is the course is being built. If it's a resort, you want a lot of pizzazz. If it's a private club, you want a good, solid, fundamentally sound golf course, and you insert bells and whistles in terms of beauty only.

By the "scale" of the golf course, I mean the size of things. Are we going to have big greens, big bunkers, sweeping fairways? Or are we going to keep things on a smaller scale? Much of that is dictated by the developer's requirements, but scale is also largely dictated by topography. If you have big, broad landforms and yawning vistas, the elements of your golf course must be big so that they match their setting. If you put little greens and little bunkers into a sprawling setting like the Summit Course at Cordillera, where you're on 190 acres at 9,000 feet and you're dealing with breathtaking views of the Rocky Mountains, the golf course will get swallowed up.

On the other hand, we are doing a golf course in Oregon called Pronghorn that is laid down in a cedar forest, so even though it has great vistas, our design elements there will be a little smaller because of the contained environment.

At this stage, it's all still pretty rough, but we are getting a good feel for the layout and for the land. If there's no variation in the vegetation, nothing really worth playing up or saving, or it's obvious that no matter how much you clear you're not going to find a great gem of nature, then the clearing may go a little faster. If that's the case, we'll go ahead and open it up and then we get down to strategy a little faster. As you can imagine, this is all very site-specific. The Bear's Club was cleared very slowly because there was so much variation in the plant life. We knew we wanted to protect a lot of that material, so we picked our way very carefully, a little bit at a time. An example of just opening up because the surrounding flora are so predictable is Pronghorn. No matter how slowly we move out, all we are going to get is cedar trees, so we can just open it up.

Throughout the development process we have a site coordinator in the field, a Nicklaus Design employee who acts as the liaison between the owner/developer, the builder, and our design office in North Palm Beach. On my site visits, my design associate and my site coordinator walk the site with me, pointing out areas where they have encountered or overcome some difficulty, and I approve or make changes. These changes are often done just by pointing and talking, but usually they're written down and sketched into topographical books that my guys carry around.

Sometimes we'll begin devising a strategy for the golf course even on these early visits. By strategy I mean the all-important, ongoing process of getting down to the precise shots that we're going to create. Sometimes strategy comes early in the game, sometimes it comes late, sometimes it gets changed in the middle, but for the sake of this discussion we'll put it here.

Strategy is where the tees go, the length of the hole, adjusting the length of a hole because it's either with or into the prevailing wind. We may need a bunker here or there. The green ought to sit at a certain angle because of a rock outcropping. Maybe there's a beautiful stream; let's make a double fairway around it with some risk-reward. That's all strategy. It may not happen on this first walk-through, but by the second or third it's usually getting pretty far along.

Sometimes I may delay getting to the strategy because of the permitting process. Rather than spend time creating hole strategies that might be rejected by local agencies for one reason or another, we'll create contour maps that give us a clear indication of the property's high and low spots. At Pronghorn I made 14 holes' worth of strategy decision on my first walk through. In that case, my guys drew the plans from scratch with the strategy I described to them. At Keene's Pointe in Orlando, we were working with a very homogenous setting, all trees. We cleared quickly and I think I gave our guy on site there the whole strategy on the spot. That can help the process, because I'm ahead of my guys as opposed to them getting a little too far down the path and me making changes.

But even in the rare instance where I can detail strategy at once, that strategy is not locked in all at once. We may put in a general strategic plan, but we'll actually implement it three or four holes at a time. The idea is to stay ahead of the construction crews,

Adjusting plans in the
field sketchbook during
an on-site visit.

but not so far ahead that we don't see the whole golf course evolve strategically. On each visit I get a little more detailed in terms of what has already been done and what I still want to do. I try to move three or four holes into the later stages of construction while bringing three or four others into the middle stages. That's when I begin to see how I want to do the bunkering, how I want to do the greens. This is the first time in the entire process that I really know the holes, so that's when I'm comfortable executing very specific details.

There is no rulebook here. Experienced golf course designers have years, even decades of design experience, but when it comes time to make the final decisions on the design elements—i.e., the shape of bunkers and greens—those decisions are made largely by the seat of your pants. It's not unlike a film director who knows the storyline and the script, but who adds his personal touch by making creative decisions based on how he thinks the story ought to be told. People don't like to hear that, it makes them think there's snake oil in the design business, but, technical as golf course design may seem, in the end it comes down to a series of creative, intuitive decisions backed up by years of experience.

I'm lucky. I don't have to rely solely on my own creativity and judgment. I have a staff of designers, some of whom have worked with me for ten and twenty years. I have ten guys in house right now who are as qualified as any designer in the country. Period. They understand that I'm the one who makes the final call regarding what goes into the ground and how it plays, but I like to give my guys freedom on stylistics as long as the aesthetics and playability and strategy of the course meet what I want. I create variety by giving my staff leeway. In some cases I have clients who specifically request that I make every single decision. I have no problem with that. It makes my job a little bit tougher, but that's okay.

With the strategy in place, we now know the places where we'll have to move some dirt. For instance, if the strategy calls for a man-made lake, a long, deep bunker or a raised or sunken green, we know we'll need to start moving. We move dirt in a variety of ways and to differing extents, all dependent upon the site. On some courses we just delicately use a bulldozer to shape the land. On some golf courses, where for one reason or another we have to move more dirt, we use scrapers. We scrape the dirt, put it in

Right: *I'm up on the ladder to get a better view. Even a few feet can make a big difference.*

Opposite: *Checking the map at the site.*

*A golf course moves
into the final stages
of clearing.*

the pans, and haul it off to another spot. You dig your man-made lakes that way, generally, and put that dirt on other parts of the course.

That's an aspect of design and construction that isn't usually recognized by the average golfer. While a site under construction might look as though we're just digging away, we always try to make sure that our cuts (digging) and fills (dumping) balance out. On our average golf course, we probably move about 250,000 yards of dirt. At Cimaron Hills in Georgetown, Texas, I think we moved less than 100,000 yards. At Bear Lakes, where we did two golf courses, each course got 250,000 yards of dirt out of its lakes. At The Bear's Club, we moved about 400,000 yards. At Dove Canyon, in Mission Viejo, California, a course I designed in 1991, we moved several million of yards of dirt.

Drainage and Irrigation

Now it's time to put in the plumbing: drainage and irrigation. The single most critical aspect in guaranteeing the quality and playability of a golf course is the control of water. Ninety-five percent of all golf course remodeling work is owing to problems with water—problems with getting it on the course and problems with getting it off the course. It's a huge part of our up-front planning. It goes back to our initial feasibility inspections. It's in our minds as we try to use the natural land formations to assist in draining or watering the course. For all of us, from the first time we put pencil to paper, we think "encourage positive drainage." It's an enormous factor in the success or failure of a golf course. But while it plays out on a huge scale with miles of pipe, it's not so very different from building a house. You need to supply it with the water you want and to protect it from the water you don't want.

In golf course design, we're always trying to figure out: Where is the water going to go? How do we make use of streams or creeks or lakes? How long would a pipe run have to be to get the water out of a certain part of the property?

Top: Wellpoints such as the ones shown here are used to draw water away from high water table areas. This one was installed at The Bear's Club in Jupiter, Florida.

Drainage goes in first. As we've seen, just about every decision you make as a golf course designer is site-specific. What works in terms of drainage for a course built in the highlands is going to differ greatly from the drainage solution for a course built in marshland. For instance, in places such as Asia or the northwestern United States, where the indigenous soil is heavy clay and they get a lot of rain, you run the risk of rainwater getting trapped between the turf and the clay. As water accumulates, it starts to seep back up through the grass, and before you know it, the golf course is closed for the day. Even though you may have positive surface drainage, meaning that the land itself is canted to assist in the flow of water, the water cannot penetrate the heavy, wet clay. The solution in these cases is to "plate" or "sand cap" the course as we did at English Turn. We cover the entire golf course with a layer of sand six to 24 inches deep, depending on the site. The sand won't saturate, but instead lets the water work down away from the grass. It will hit the clay eventually, but will travel along it to a drain tile and then into a pipe and out.

Once the drainage problems are resolved, we move on to irrigation. If there is a real estate development involved, we get our master drainage set and then string the sewer lines. It is critical to get the fundamental heavy earthwork done before you start your plumbing. I've seen numerous projects where the sewer plans were changed for one reason or another and the golf course had to be ripped up—across the fairways and through the trees—and it just cripples a project.

Once we've finished clearing, we'll move whatever dirt the plans require. We'll rough-shape and grade four to six holes, and then I'll make another visit. If I've already given the strategy, then I'm looking to see if the scale, theme, and design of the bunkers, greens, and fairways are what I had in mind. If I haven't yet given the strategy, this is when I start to insert it. I'll look over the hole and add the strategic elements, adding a bunker here, putting a mound there.

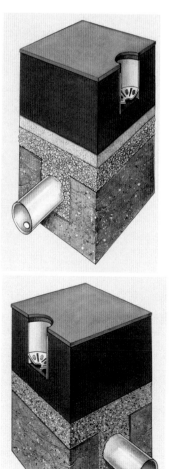

Then we build our greens and tees. If there's one thing that the average golfer doesn't know about golf course design, it's how complex the substructure is. This is true of the entire golf course, the substructure of which is lined with so many layers of drainage and pipes and hoses, but it's particularly true of the greens.

Like most professional golf course design firms, most of our greens are built according to USGA specifications. The USGA has a division called the Green Section that since 1920 has been the game's authoritative source for information on turf management. The specs they issue for how to build a green that can sustain heavy traffic, drain efficiently, and provide a consistently good playing surface have been adopted by all serious golf course designers. While the specs themselves are quite technical, we can take a simplified look at a cross-section of a typical USGA green.

Beneath the grassy playing surface is the substructure for a green. The substructure is based on the Perched Water

Table theory, which holds that water will not move from one medium to another until the first medium is saturated. A green begins with a vertical cut 16 inches deep. The first four inches are pea gravel with tile laid in a herringbone pattern. Sometimes we put in a two-inch choker layer of very small gravel and then 12 inches of sand and some organic (usually peat) mix.

With all these steps complete, shaping is nearly done and it's time for finish work. Finish work is where we try to get the land back to what it looked like before we got there. We try to get the flow lines right and to make the land look as natural as possible.

As important as the finished look is, accuracy at this point is even more vital. In finish

Left: Laser levelers such as the one shown here are used to determine the accuracy of the grading and leveling done in the final shaping.

Below: As the finish work comes to an end, the course is ready for grassing.

The bunker is prepared for sand and grassing.

work an inch is important—even a half-inch can be critical. For example, if the final grade of a fairway is off an inch, maintenance will be difficult and expensive. It can also mean that the drainage that was installed beneath that fairway may not have the capacity to handle the amount of water it will now receive.

Finished shaping is also critical from an aesthetic standpoint, but it's usually reflective of the quality of the rough shaping that was done earlier. Rough shaping is the broad strokes, the movement of perhaps thousands of tons of dirt and the creation of the golf course's scale. If that part is not done correctly, all the short strokes in the world can't fix it. Throughout the process, we are aided by the unsung heroes of golf course design—the shapers. Golf course design is essentially a journey from the general to the specific. From the time we begin what we call rough shaping, down to the final inch, we rely on shapers to translate the design vision from paper into reality. Their guidelines come both from the topo instructions and from stakes that we put in the ground all

Here I have just thrown a ball to test the sand in a bunker. You can see the ball at the far left. I like to use a sand that will drain but set up firm, so that the ball won't bury easily. This was a test bunker built at The Bear's Club. It was in place prior to Hurricane Irene (23 inches of rain). It didn't move an inch and percolated beautifully.

Opposite: grass can be installed in a variety of ways. In addition to seeding and sodding, we often use a procedure called sprigging, in which grass stolons are inserted into the soil. The machine rigged to the tractor is a sprigger, which punches the stolons into the soil.

Left: Before a machine can sprig an area, we hand-sprinkle the stolons on the surface.

*Here the foreground
has been sodded and
the middle ground
has been sprigged.*

The photos on these pages show the transformation of a neglected piece of land in Dearborn, Michigan into the award-winning TPC of Michigan. At far right is the finished 10th hole.

over the property that are marked to show just how high up on each stake the earth should be. That may not sound too hard until you realize that these guys, mostly freelancers, are doing it on top of 3-ton bulldozers. It's sort of like asking Michelangelo to sculpt with a telephone pole. Most designers have a handful of shapers they use regularly. I rely on mine every day to understand my vision and translate it accurately to the final product. The shapers' ability to translate the design team's vision is vital, and ultimately it's their touch that makes the golf course a golf course.

With all that behind us, it's time to plant grass and watch the course take shape. The three basic methods of grassing a course are sodding, sprigging, and seeding. In sodding, living patches of grass are essentially grafted onto the course's soil. In sprigging, stolons (stems of grass plants) are sprinkled throughout an area and plugged with a sprigging machine (sprigger). Seeding is self-explanatory.

7 The Next Generation

In the early 1990s, the members of the American Society of Golf Course Architects were asked to identify the most significant problem facing their business. The answer was not zoning approvals or wetlands law or even the economic recession we were then experiencing. Ninety-three percent said their biggest problem was the increasing distance that golf balls were traveling.

That was more than a decade ago, when even avid golfers had not yet fully embraced modern shaft and clubhead technology. Ball manufacturers were still on the cusp of breakthroughs that allowed balls to travel longer and control spin better.

Today it has all come together. We are seeing quantum leaps in clubhead technology, golf course maintenance technology, and ball technology. But in my opinion, the biggest "advances" have been made by the golf ball.

The bad news is that the ball is an enormous problem. The good news is it's the one thing we can really try to control. You can control the golf club a bit, but you match up balls and clubs today and we all hit the ball straighter than we deserve to. I make so

Watching my birdie putt on the 17th hole of the final round at the 1986 Masters. Advances in golf ball technology have led Augusta National to make some dramatic changes.

many bad swings today and look up and the ball goes straight. And everybody else does the same thing. Today, a tour player should nearly never be in the rough. If he doesn't hit 10 out of 14 fairways or 11 out of 14 fairways, he's having a pretty bad driving day. We used to think that was a pretty good driving day. This is basically the result of technology allowing the club to be very forgiving. And when the golf club is forgiving, you can go ahead and just swing away.

What happened? Manufacturers have finally figured out how to make a hard ball playable. Remember those "rocks" that used to go forever? Well, now the "rock" is a playable golf ball, even more playable than some of the old soft balls we used to play. If the ball was a problem ten years ago, it's a real threat now. The USGA's numbers show that golf ball distance increased about a yard per year from the early 1980s to the mid 1990s. Then, in the last three or four years, distance has grown by about five yards per year.

Symptoms of this crisis are currently surfacing at the professional tour level. If a golf course is too short for the average golfer, he usually has another tee to move back to. The pros don't have that option. They're already playing from the tips, so you've got to build new tees every few years until you run out of room or money, whichever comes first. The long ball also has a negative effect on tournament set-ups. It forces tournament committees to protect par in *some* way, and what they'll generally do is put the pins in more awkward positions. Others say: Maybe there's something courses can do with their greens to balance out the ball? I think they already do. Look at Augusta. Look at the pin placements today versus the pin placements from 30 years ago. We would have laughed 30 years ago if you had said you were going to put the pins in some of today's locations. Look at Pinehurst No. 2, when we played the U.S. Open there in 1999. They expanded the greens and ended up putting half the pins on the roll-offs. That was never part of Donald Ross's vision—the USGA was just trying to find ways to counter the ball.

Sometimes they'll redesign the green in order to get more awkward positions, but ultimately you're left with the same problem: You're going to run out of money or space eventually, and the ball is going to lap you. In a discussion with some golf writers not too long ago, I was asked what professional golf would be like in 50 years. I said, "I assume we'll just tee off from our hotels."

So what is a tournament golf course to do? Look at Augusta National. They have been struggling with this issue since 1997, when Tiger Woods rewrote the record book in his inaugural win. Look at all the work they did over the summer and fall of 2001. Personally, I understand what they're doing. They did similar things to rein me in during my heyday. Back in the 1960s and 1970s:

They moved the first tee back, but they also moved the fairway bunker back to where it would be in play.

They put the bunker in at No. 2.

They moved the tee back at No. 8 so that the fairway bunker would be in play.

They moved the tee back at No. 9 because I was playing a sand wedge into the green.

They put the mounds in along the 15th hole and the bunkers in at No. 18 to control me.

Sure, I think Augusta could use a little more length, but eventually adding length is a losing proposition. All golf courses have their limits. I think Augusta should focus more on accuracy. They should stay what they are, a second-shot golf course, and force the field to play accurate second shots. That's what they did when I was young. They forced me to hit the ball straighter.

I think they are making Tiger and other long hitters hit the ball longer and straighter, but they are totally eliminating anyone who can hit the ball straight but can't hit it long. They're moving the tees back on Nos. 1, 7, 8, 9, 10, 11, 13, 14, and 18, and forcing everyone to compete with Tiger's length. That's only going to help Tiger or any very long hitter. The longer the course, the more advantage they have.

What would I do? I'm not sure, but I would try very hard not to change the character of the course and the tournament that Bob Jones created. The Masters is my favorite tournament in all of golf, and I hope they end up preserving all its great traditions.

In 1993, we were only hearing about this problem from golf course architects, who were the first to see the effect that the longer ball was having on great old designs. Look at Merion. It's one of the great old golf courses in this country, but at 6,500 yards from the tips and 6,100 from the middle tees, it's been bypassed by the ball. It can never host another major professional championship. That's a serious loss for the game.

St. Andrews is already obsolete. The ball goes so much farther now that today's players just are not facing the same golf course we did. Is Tiger Woods playing the same

St. Andrews that I played throughout my career? Not even close. With the distance the golf ball now travels, he didn't have a single bunker in play. People marvel at the fact that in his 2000 British Open win, Tiger did not hit any bunkers. Nothing at all against Tiger, but there was no bunker in play for him, nor was there for a fairly large group of players. I won twice there and I assure you that every bunker was fully in play. In fact, my strategy for winning at St. Andrews was based on avoiding bunkers with smart, accurate shots.

You can scramble and tweak some courses to fend off the ball for a few years, but St. Andrews is out of room. They're done. And other courses will be too.

The ball is clearly the biggest issue confronting golf course designers and developers right now. Manufacturers have found a way to stay within the rules of the USGA's "Iron Byron" conformity tests but still deliver massive amounts of distance in the hands of professional golfers. That will eventually trickle down to the club-level player who, over time, will either lose interest in a golf course that no longer challenges him or get fed up with the continual assessments required to lengthen his course every two years in order to keep it relevant. The thing that worries me is that I don't know how far this thing is going to go before the USGA or the PGA Tour takes action. In the meantime, we just keep lengthening and lengthening golf courses.

What should we do? I agree with Arnold Palmer that the game should be fun for the amateur golfer. The rules as they are are fine for the amateur. The average kid or the average weekend foursome have fun hitting the golf ball longer and it brings people into the game. But for the showcase events, such as PGA Tour events, USGA championships, and the other majors, let every manufacturer make a golf ball that's 10 percent shorter. If we take just 10 percent off the golf ball's distance, we bring hundreds of great golf courses back from the brink of extinction. Instead of needing 7,200-yard courses to challenge the top professionals, you'd only need 6,500 yards. How many great 6,500-yard golf courses are there in the United States? Hundreds. Easily 100 courses could again be considered as hosts for the U.S. Open if you brought the ball back 10 percent. And you have thousands of courses at risk of obsolescence if the ball *picks up* another 10 percent, which it's clearly going to do.

Tiger Woods at the 2000 U. S. Open at Pebble Beach. Tiger is the greatest player in golf today. The combination of his power and skill and the technology of modern golf balls is threatening the relevance of many great championship tests.

All equipment, particularly the golf balls, has undergone a dramatic evolution in the last 150 years. After the feather-filled balls of golf's early days came the breakthrough latex gutta percha ball. Then came hammered balls; the bramble ball (so named for its resemblance to a berry); the Haskell rubber ball; and eventually, today's marvels of technology.

Take the golf ball I was playing in 2000. According to USGA testing, it was the longest legal ball on the market. One year later, it was not even considered a long ball. Technology completely passed it by in a few short months. If this keeps up, all we'll have left is memories of today's great courses. It's sad.

The shorter ball can have the same aerodynamics, the same advertising, the same everything. A ball company that signs Tiger Woods because he is so long will still be able to make that claim. Even if we bring the ball back 10 percent, Tiger is still going to hit it 20 yards past most of the guys out there. It's just that if we do bring the ball back, we won't be rendering great old championship layouts obsolete for professional tournament golf.

The PGA Tour would have to support such a move, but they're in a difficult spot. If they tried to mandate a shorter ball, they'd have every manufacturer in the country take them to court. And they'd have every tour player battling them. But if the USGA steps in first and establishes the shorter ball as a Rule of the Game they'd get some static, but I think the PGA Tour—specifically its policy board, which has the final say on such issues—would support them. Together, they could prevail. Another option is the golf course owners of America. They have the most to lose. Banded together, they might possibly get the ball under control.

Why hasn't the USGA or the PGA Tour limited the ball? Mostly fear. But you cannot let the golf ball threaten great courses simply because some ball manufacturer threatens a lawsuit. It just doesn't make any sense to stand by and allow the golf ball to follow the course it's on. If we do, I think we're robbing the future of the past's greatest courses. I tip my hat to Augusta National for taking a leadership role in March 2002, when they said they'd be open to the idea of requiring a special ball for the Masters.

We've seen it at Muirfield Village too. In recent years, Tiger has played this hole with a 3-wood off the tee and his second shot into the 11th green (one of my "unreachable" par-5s) with a 2-iron. The only thing I saw to do there was to lengthen the hole a little and make the tee shot a little more demanding. If somebody still wants to go ahead and hit a driver down there, I'm not going to keep him from getting home.

We changed No. 15 a year ago. Before, you could just hit it anywhere left of the green. It was a fairly easy pitch shot. I don't mind them making eagles and birdies, but a guy who hits a bad tee shot ought at least to be confronted with the *possibility* of making bogey. Conversely, a guy who hits a good tee shot has got a chance for birdie or eagle. I wanted to keep that. But I wanted to make it not quite so easy.

I don't think that anything we've done to Muirfield over the last two or three years was done specifically for Tiger. What we did at 11 or 15 certainly isn't going to affect Tiger. Those changes affect how you play the hole in general, not how *he* plays the hole. I don't believe you can "Tiger-proof" a golf course. What we're trying to do is bring the hazards into play for more players, so the course requires better golf. If you do that well, length becomes less of an issue. The focus becomes putting the ball in play.

People ask if the conditioning of today's courses also encourages better bounces, longer rolls, and lower scores. Improved conditioning is certainly a factor. I do not think it's the biggest factor. We had well-conditioned golf courses 30 years ago. Not all of them were, but certainly Firestone Country Club was always wonderfully conditioned. When we played at Augusta, it was always in great condition. The U.S. Open was always good. The PGA Championship was always good. The British Open was always good.

It's no longer a question of protecting par, it's a question of protecting the golf course. The golfers are probably better today. Equipment is better. The golf ball goes farther. So they shoot lower scores, so what? I don't have a problem with that. The only problem I have is when none of the difficulty ever comes into play. I have done 11 golf courses for one of my clients. One of those courses is only two years old. He came to me recently and said, "Jack, you did 11 courses for me in the last 15 years. They were all great. Now they're are all obsolete."

How can you build a golf course and two years later it's obsolete?

In my opinion, the future of golf course design looks quite different from its past. A lot of the problems addressed in this book will be exacerbated. Environmentally, developers and designers will face more and more sensitive situations. They will be able to use less and less of the ground on hand, and be required to work around many more restrictions.

As the years go by, fewer magnificent sites will be available. Instead of beautiful coastal views and mountain vistas, a lot of the ground that golf course designers will be presented with in the next 20, 50, 100 years will be distressed. By that I mean that there will be more rehabilitation of heavily polluted or otherwise troubled sites. More courses will be built in unlikely settings, such as tapped-out gravel pits and quarries. As we start to run out of developable natural coastline, you'll see more courses built entirely on fill. The groundbreaking work we did at Old Works Golf Club in Anaconda, Montana, points the way.

Imagination has always been integral to quality design. I think the future will place a premium on golf course design (and other land planning) that goes "outside the box" and adapts to new needs.

Beyond the coming shortage of spectacular land, there will be less land to work with overall. We've talked about the challenge presented by the longer balls and the clubs behind them. Designers as a group have to convince developers and club members to keep their courses at reasonable lengths. If courses grow longer as available land shrinks, inescapable conflicts will arise.

Those are the key environmental and land-planning issues that will confront designers in the twenty-first century, and like any problem a designer encounters in the course of a project, they can be resolved. The solutions 50 years from now will only be as good as the designers who then inhabit the business. That's where I draw my confidence in the future of golf course architecture.

There has never been a shortage of talent in this business. You know the names: Pete Dye, Tom Fazio, Robert Trent Jones and his sons, Rees and Robert Trent Jones II, Morrish, Cupp, Weiskopf, Palmer, Player, Hills. Before them came Bell, Bendelow, Braid, Tillinghast, Ross, Colt, George Crump, Alison, Raynor, Macdonald, Mackenzie. Each found his own way into the business, often through an unrelated profession. Macdonald was a stockbroker throughout much of his design career and never accepted a penny for design services. Crump was a hotelier by trade, who designed only one golf course in his short life—the famed Pine Valley Golf Club. Pete Dye's story is well known.

As talented as these men were, I think modern golf course design has benefited from an improvement in the depth of training, both organized and ad hoc, that our young people are getting. The result is a professionalization of the field that bodes very well for the future.

Left: With my sons (from left to right) Gary, Jackie, and Steve. Each is an accomplished golf course designer in his own right.

Above: My youngest son, Michael, has recently entered the business.

Take Pete, one of the leading and most influential golf course designers in the country. He came out of the insurance industry and rocketed to the top. That worked in an era when we had fewer land-planning and environmental and chemical and agronomical issues to worry about. Same with me. I brought with me years of playing and competitive experience, but in the 21st and 22nd centuries, that may not be enough.

Most of our young staffers at Nicklaus Design, including most of my family, have started the best way I know how: in the field. They've packed up and gone to sites, actually lived on them, taken their families there. First they work in construction, then they learn about design. As a design coordinator, they go through every headache the project goes through, whether it is environmental, construction, irrigation, or drainage. They see the problems first-hand. To a large extent, they get down there and dig out the solutions themselves.

A high percentage of the aspiring designers we have in our office have college degrees in landscape architecture or turf sciences. But whether they have the degree or not, they all work their way up the ladder we've established. They start as design coordinators, then move up to design associate, where they work in the office on our drawings. Then there's a transition step where they're design coordinator/design associate, in which they not only work on drawings under me but also on coordination with the owner and the contractor. Ultimately, they become a design associate, a full-fledged golf course designer working under me. Sometimes our DAs take their training and go off on their own, sometimes they stay with me for decades.

I think this is a fine way to learn the business. I think my son Jackie is better trained than I am. Second son Steve has done several courses, every one of which has gotten solid reviews. My son-in-law, Bill O'Leary, who grew up knowing nothing about the game, has put in so much time in the field and has acquired so much practical on-site knowledge that he's gotten very good. Like successful people in any field, he's smart enough to ask questions. As Bill continues to mature as a designer, so does his reputation in the industry. One of the more recent projects Bill was involved in, Whispering Pines Golf Club in Trinity, Texas, was selected by *Golf Digest* as third among the Best New Private Courses in America for 2000. Son Gary came into the business the same way I did, as a player first, and he has done some very good design work. One of his courses, the Prospector Course at Superstition Mountain, recently hosted The Tradition, a major on the Senior PGA Tour. Michael, our youngest, is just starting out. Right now he's doing a lot of work on the computer. Given how far he hits the ball, we ought to have him specialize in the long courses. Maybe he'll be the designer who builds a golf course long enough to contain him.

What does it mean to have sons in the business with me? It's really neat. Jackie, who has been doing a lot of work on my designs with me lately, recently took a solo trip to South Carolina, where we are in the final stages of construction on a course. Two holes still needed work. When he got back, he popped his head in my office and said, "We got No. 1 and No. 18 done, and I adjusted one of the bunkers on 18 from a visibility standpoint after what we discussed last week." It's exciting to see that seamless transition between his work and mine.

Having sons in the business also gives me a sense of continuity. I'm delighted that my family is interested enough and talented enough to take some of the load and to deal with it so expertly. It's pretty nice to have my family not only want to do it, but to have the same interests you have in the first place.

My son-in-law, Bill O'Leary, is an up-and-coming young designer.

The design business has been a real blessing for me. It started as an avocation, just for fun—in fact, a lot of my early jobs cost ME money. In retrospect, it was like paying for an education.

I never could have guessed, back in 1965, that a walk in the woods with Pete Dye would put me where I am today. Since then it's been a lot of work, hundreds of thousands of miles traveled, but always thoroughly enjoyable. Even now, when I struggle with my golf game, design keeps me close to the sport I love. I've been able to make money at it, and to meet fascinating people all over the world. It gets me outdoors in all seasons, which I love. My work has been singled out for honors and my courses have been ranked (they've also been criticized, but that's fair). It keeps me young, and it keeps me close to my family. But the best part of being a golf course designer is knowing that the courses I design today will be around long after I'm gone. I hope they serve as living, growing testimonials to my love of the game.

Courses Open for Play as of March, 2002

CLUB NAME	LOCATION	DESIGNER/CO-DESIGNER/YEAR
Alabang Golf & Country Club	Alabang, Muntinlupa, The Philippines	Nicklaus Design, 1999
Aliso Viejo Golf Club	Aliso Viejo, CA	Jack Nicklaus, Jack Nicklaus II, 1999
Annandale Golf Club	Jackson, MS	Jack Nicklaus (Signature), 1981
Arzaga Golf Club	Drugolo di Lonato, Brescia, Italy	Jack Nicklaus II, 1998
Aspen Glen Golf Club	Carbondale, CO	Jack Nicklaus, Jack Nicklaus II, 1997
Aston Oaks	North Bend, OH	Nicklaus Design, 1999
Atlanta Country Club	Marietta, GA	Jack Nicklaus, 1983 (Redesign)
Australian Golf Club	Rosebery, New South Wales, Australia,	Jack Nicklaus, 1977 (Redesign)
Avila Golf & Country Club	Tampa, FL	Jack Nicklaus, 1989 (Redesign)
Ballantrae Golf & Yacht Club	Port St. Lucie, FL	Jack Nicklaus (Signature), 1993
Barrington Golf Club	Aurora, OH	Jack Nicklaus (Signature), 1994
Bear Creek Golf Club	Murrieta, CA	Jack Nicklaus (Signature), 1982
Bear Creek Golf Course at Chandler – Long Course	Chandler, AZ	Bill O'Leary, 2000
Bear Creek Golf Course at Chandler – Short Course	Chandler, AZ	Bill O'Leary, 2001
Bear Lakes Country Club – Lakes Course	West Palm Beach, FL	Jack Nicklaus (Signature), 1985
Bear Lakes Country Club – Links Course	West Palm Beach, FL	Jack Nicklaus (Signature), 1988
The Bear Trace at Chickasaw	Henderson, TN	Jack Nicklaus (Signature), 2000
The Bear Trace at Cumberland Mountain	Crossville, TN	Jack Nicklaus (Signature), 1998
The Bear Trace at Harrison Bay	Harrison, TN	Jack Nicklaus (Signature), 1999
The Bear Trace at Ross Creek	Clifton, TN	Jack Nicklaus (Signature), 2001
The Bear Trace at Tims Ford	Winchester, TN	Jack Nicklaus (Signature), 1999
Bearpath Golf & Country Club	Eden Prairie, MN	Jack Nicklaus (Signature), 1996
Bear's Best Las Vegas	Las Vegas, NV	Jack Nicklaus (Signature Compilation), 2001
The Bear's Club	Jupiter, FL	Jack Nicklaus (Signature), 2000
Bear's Paw Golf Club	Naples, FL	Jack Nicklaus (Signature), 1980
Bear's Paw Japan	Kouga-gun, Shiga, Japan	Jack Nicklaus (Signature), 2000
Bintan Lagoon Resort & Country Club	Bintan Island, Indonesia	Jack Nicklaus (Signature), 1997
Birch River (Nicklaus Golf Club at)	Dahlonega, GA	Jack Nicklaus (Signature), 2000
Borneo Golf & Country Club	Bogawan, Sabah, Malaysia	Jack Nicklaus (Signature), 1995
Breckenridge, 3rd Nine	Breckenridge, CO	Jack Nicklaus (Signature), 2001
Breckenridge Golf Club	Breckenridge, CO	Jack Nicklaus (Signature), 1987
Britannia Golf and Beach Club	Grand Cayman, Cayman Islands, BWI	Jack Nicklaus (Signature), 1985

CLUB NAME	LOCATION	DESIGNER/CO-DESIGNER/YEAR
Bukit Barisan Country Club at Medan	Medan, Indonesia	Jack Nicklaus (Signature), 1996
Bukit Darmo Golf Club	Surabaya, Indonesia	Jack Nicklaus II, 1995
Cabo del Sol – Ocean Course	Cabo San Lucas, Baja California Sur, Mexico	Jack Nicklaus (Signature), 1994
Camp John Hay	Bagio, Benguet, The Philippines	Nicklaus Design, 1999
Carden Park	Cheshire, England	Jack Nicklaus, Steve Nicklaus, 1998
Castle Pines Golf Club	Castle Rock, CO	Jack Nicklaus (Signature), 1981
Castlewoods Country Club	Brandon, MS	Nicklaus Design, 1994
Challenge at Manele	Lanai City, HI	Jack Nicklaus (Signature), 1993
Chang An Golf & Country Club	Taipei, Taiwan	Jack Nicklaus (Signature), 1993
Chung Shan Hot Spring Golf Club	Zongshan City, China	Jack Nicklaus (Signature), 1993
Classic Golf Resort	New Delhi, India	Jack Nicklaus (Signature), 1998
The Club at Carlton Woods	The Woodlands, TX	Jack Nicklaus (Signature), 2001
The Club at Morningside	Rancho Mirage, CA	Jack Nicklaus (Signature), 1981
The Club at Nevillewood	Nevillewood, PA	Jack Nicklaus (Signature), 1992
The Club at Porto Cima	Lake of the Ozarks, MO	Jack Nicklaus (Signature), 2000
The Club at TwinEagles – Talon Course	Naples, FL	Jack Nicklaus, Jack Nicklaus II, 1999
La Moraleja Golf Club	Madrid, Alcobendas, Spain	Jack Nicklaus, Desmond Muirhead, 1976
Colleton River Plantation	Hilton Head Island, SC	Jack Nicklaus (Signature), 1992
The Club at Castle Pines	Castle Rock, CO	Jack Nicklaus (Signature), 1986
The Country Club at Muirfield	Dublin, OH	Jack Nicklaus (Signature), 1982
Country Club Bosques	Mexico City, Mexico	Nicklaus Design, 1996
Country Club Khao Yai	Nahkon Ratchasima, Thailand	Jack Nicklaus (Signature), 1994
Country Club of Landfall	Wilmington, NC	Jack Nicklaus (Signature), 1990
Country Club of Landfall 9 holes	Wilmington, NC	Jack Nicklaus (Signature), 2000
Country Club of Louisiana	Baton Rouge, LA	Jack Nicklaus (Signature), 1986
Country Club of the North	Beavercreek, OH	Jack Nicklaus (Signature), 1993
Country Club of the Rockies	Edwards, CO	Jack Nicklaus (Signature), 1984
Country Club of the South	Alpharetta, GA	Jack Nicklaus (Signature), 1987
Coyote Creek Golf Club– Valley Course	San Jose, CA	Jack Nicklaus, 2001
Coyote Creek	Peoria, IL	Nicklaus Design, 2001
Coyote Creek Golf Club – Tournament Course	San Jose, CA	Jack Nicklaus (Signature), 1999
Cozumel Country Club	Cozumel, Quintana Roo, Mexico	Nicklaus Design featuring Steve Nicklaus, 2001

CLUB NAME	LOCATION	DESIGNER/CO-DESIGNER/YEAR
Dallas Athletic Club – Blue Course	Dallas, TX	Jack Nicklaus, 1986 (Redesign)
Dallas Athletic Club – Gold Course	Dallas, TX	Jack Nicklaus, 1989 (Redesign)
Damai Indah Golf & Country Club	Jakarta, Indonesia	Jack Nicklaus (Signature), 1992
Daufuskie Island Club & Resort/Melrose	Hilton Head, SC	Jack Nicklaus (Signature), 1987
Desert Highlands Golf Club	Scottsdale, AZ	Jack Nicklaus (Signature), 1984
Desert Mountain – Apache	Scottsdale, AZ	Jack Nicklaus (Signature), 1996
Desert Mountain – Chiricahua	Scottsdale, AZ	Jack Nicklaus (Signature), 1999
Desert Mountain – Cochise	Scottsdale, AZ	Jack Nicklaus (Signature), 1988
Desert Mountain – Geronimo	Scottsdale, AZ	Jack Nicklaus (Signature), 1989
Desert Mountain – Renegade	Scottsdale, AZ	Jack Nicklaus (Signature), 1987
Dove Canyon Country Club	Dove Canyon, CA	Jack Nicklaus (Signature), 1991
Eagle Bend Golf Course	Big Fork, MT	Jack Nicklaus II, 1995
Eldorado Golf Club	Los Cabos, Mexico	Jack Nicklaus (Signature), 1999
Elk River Club	Banner Elk, NC	Jack Nicklaus (Signature), 1984
Emeralda Golf & Country Club	Cimanngis, Bogor, Indonesia	Jack Nicklaus (Signature), 1995
English Turn Golf & Country Club	New Orleans, LA	Jack Nicklaus (Signature), 1988
Estrella Mountain Ranch Golf Club	Goodyear, AZ	Jack Nicklaus II, 1999
Forest Hills Golf and Country Club	Inarawan, Antipolo, The Philippines	Jack Nicklaus II, 1997
Four Seasons Golf Club Punta Mita	Punta Mita, Mexico	Jack Nicklaus (Signature), 1999
Gapyeong Benest Golf Club	Gapyeong-gun, Kyunggi-do, South Korea	Jack Nicklaus (Signature), 2000
Gapyeong Benest Golf Club 9 holes	Gapyeong-gun, Kyunggi-do, South Korea	Nicklaus Design, 2000
Glen Abbey Golf Club	Oakville, Ontario, Canada	Jack Nicklaus (Signature), 1976
Gleneagles Hotel, The PGA Centenary Course	Perthshire, Scotland	Jack Nicklaus (Signature), 1993
Glenmoor Country Club	Canton, OH	Jack Nicklaus (Signature), 1992
Golden Bear Club at Indigo Run	Hilton Head Island, SC	Nicklaus Design, 1993
Golf Center at Kings Island – Bruin	Mason, OH	Jack Nicklaus, Desmond Muirhead, 1973
Golf Center at Kings Island – Grizzly	Mason, OH	Jack Nicklaus, Desmond Muirhead, 1973
The Golf Club at Indigo Run	Hilton Head Island, SC	Jack Nicklaus, Jack Nicklaus II, 1995
The Golf Club at Mansion Ridge	Monroe, NY	Jack Nicklaus (Signature), 1999
Golf Club Crans-sur-Sierre	Crans-sur-Sierre, Switzerland	Jack Nicklaus (Signature), 1988
The Golf Club of Purchase	Purchase, NY	Jack Nicklaus (Signature), 1996
Golf Platz Gut Larchenhof	Cologne, Germany	Jack Nicklaus (Signature), 1997

CLUB NAME	LOCATION	DESIGNER/CO-DESIGNER/YEAR
Governors Club	Chapel Hill, NC	Jack Nicklaus (Signature), 1990
Grand Bear	Saucier, MS	Jack Nicklaus (Signature), 1999
Grand Cypress GC – New	Orlando, FL	Jack Nicklaus (Signature), 1988
Grand Cypress Golf Club (North, South, East)	Orlando, FL	Jack Nicklaus (Signature), 1984
Grand Geneva Resort	Lake Geneva, WI	Jack Nicklaus, Pete Dye, 1970
Grand Haven Golf Club	Palm Coast, FL	Jack Nicklaus (Signature), 1998
Grand Traverse Resort – The Bear	Acme, MI	Jack Nicklaus (Signature), 1984
Great Bear Golf & Country Club	Shawnee on Delaware, PA	Jack Nicklaus (Signature), 1997
Great Waters at Reynolds Plantation	Greensboro, GA	Jack Nicklaus (Signature), 1992
The Greenbrier Course	White Sulphur Springs, WV	Jack Nicklaus, 1978 (Redesign)
Gut Altentann Golf & Country Club	Salzburg, Austria	Jack Nicklaus (Signature), 1988
Hammock Creek Golf Club	Palm City, FL	Jack Nicklaus, Jack Nicklaus II, 1996
Hananomori Golf Club	Ohira, Miyagi, Japan	Jack Nicklaus (Signature), 1992
Hanbury Manor	London, England	Jack Nicklaus II, 1991
Harbour Town Golf Links	Hilton Head, SC	Jack Nicklaus, Pete Dye, 1970
Heritage Golf & Country Club	Melbourne, Victoria, Australia	Jack Nicklaus (Signature), 2000
The Hertfordshire Golf & Country Club	Broxbourne, Hertfordshire, England	Nicklaus Design, 1996
Hibiki no Mori Country Club	Kurabuchi, Gunma, Japan	Jack Nicklaus (Signature), 1996
Hills Country Club (The)	Austin, TX	Jack Nicklaus (Signature), 1981
Hokkaido Classic	Hayakita, Hokkaido, Japan	Jack Nicklaus (Signature), 1991
Hualalai Golf Club	Kailua-Kona, HI	Jack Nicklaus (Signature), 1996
Huis Ten Bosch Country Club	Seihi, Nagasaki, Japan	Jack Nicklaus (Signature), 1992
Ibis Golf & Country Club - Heritage	West Palm Beach, FL	Jack Nicklaus II, 1991
Ibis Golf & Country Club - Legend	West Palm Beach, FL	Jack Nicklaus (Signature), 1991
Ibis Golf & Country Club - Tradition	West Palm Beach, FL	Steve Nicklaus, 2001
Ishioka Golf Club	Ogawa, Ibaraki, Japan	Jack Nicklaus (Signature), 1994
J&P Golf Club	Utsonomiya, Tochigi, Japan	Jack Nicklaus (Signature), 1998
James Island	Victoria, British Columbia, Canada	Jack Nicklaus (Signature), 1997
Japan Memorial Golf Club	Kobe, Hyogo, Japan	Jack Nicklaus (Signature), 1990
Jerudong Golf Club	Jerudong, Brunei	Jack Nicklaus (Signature), 1998
John's Island/South Course	Vero Beach, FL	Jack Nicklaus, Pete Dye, 1970
Kauai Lagoons – Kiele Course	Lihue, HI	Jack Nicklaus (Signature), 1988

CLUB NAME	LOCATION	DESIGNER/CO-DESIGNER/YEAR
Kauai Lagoons – Mokihana Course	Lihue, HI	Jack Nicklaus (Signature), 1989
Keene's Pointe (The Golden Bear Club at)	Windermere, FL	Jack Nicklaus (Signature), 1999
King & Bear	St. Augustine, FL	Jack Nicklaus, Arnold Palmer, 2000
Komono Golf Club	Komono, Mie, Japan	Jack Nicklaus (Signature), 1992
La Gorce Country Club	Miami Beach, FL	Jack Nicklaus, 1995 (Redesign)
La Paloma Country Club	Tucson, AZ	Jack Nicklaus (Signature), 1984
Laem Chabang International Country Club	Sriracha, Chonburi, Thailand	Jack Nicklaus (Signature), 1993
Lakelands Golf Club	Gold Coast, Queensland, Australia	Jack Nicklaus (Signature), 1996
Las Campanas – Sunrise	Santa Fe, NM	Jack Nicklaus (Signature), 1993
Las Campanas – Sunset	Santa Fe, NM	Jack Nicklaus (Signature), 2000
Laurel Springs Golf Club	Suwanee, GA	Jack Nicklaus (Signature), 1998
Le Robinie Golf & Sporting Club	Solbiate, Italy	Jack Nicklaus (Signature), 1995
Legacy Golf Links	Aberdeen, NC	Jack Nicklaus II, 1991
The Legends Golf & Country Club Resort	Kula, Johor, Malaysia	Jack Nicklaus (Signature), 1997
Legends West at Diablo Grande	Patterson, CA	Jack Nicklaus, Gene Sarazen, 1998
LeoPalace Resort Manenggon Hills	Barrigada, GMF, Guam	Jack Nicklaus (Signature), 1993
LionsGate (Nicklaus Golf Club at)	Overland Park, KS	Jack Nicklaus (Signature), 2001
Lochinvar Golf Club	Houston, TX	Jack Nicklaus (Signature), 1980
The London Golf Club, The Heritage	Kent, England	Jack Nicklaus (Signature), 1994
The London Golf Club International Course	Kent, England	Nicklaus Design, 1994
The Long Bay Club	North Myrtle Beach, SC	Jack Nicklaus (Signature), 1989
The Loxahatchee Club	Jupiter, FL	Jack Nicklaus (Signature), 1984
Manila Southwoods Golf & Country Club – Legends	Carmona, Cavite, The Philippines	Jack Nicklaus (Signature), 1992
Manila Southwoods Golf & Country Club – Masters	Carmona, Cavite, The Philippines	Jack Nicklaus (Signature), 1993
Mayacama Golf Club	Santa Rosa, CA	Jack Nicklaus (Signature), 2001
Mayacoo Lakes Country Club	West Palm Beach, FL	Jack Nicklaus, Desmond Muirhead, 1973
The Medallion Club	Westerville, OH	Jack Nicklaus II, 1993
Meridian Golf Club	Englewood, CO	Jack Nicklaus (Signature), 1984
Miramar Linkou Golf & Country Club	Taipei, Taiwan	Jack Nicklaus (Signature), 1994
Mission Hills Golf Club	Kanchanaburi Province, Thailand	Jack Nicklaus (Signature), 1991

CLUB NAME	LOCATION	DESIGNER/CO-DESIGNER/YEAR
Mission Hills Khao Yai Golf Club	Pakchong, Nakorn Ratchasrima, Thailand	Jack Nicklaus (Signature), 1993
Mission Hills Golf Club, Mountain Course	Guanlan Town, Shenzhen, China	Jack Nicklaus (Signature), 1994
Mission Hills Golf Club, World Cup Course	Guanlan Town, Shenzhen, China	Jack Nicklaus (Signature), 1995
Montecastillo Hotel & Golf Resort	Jerez de la Frontera, Cadiz, Spain	Jack Nicklaus (Signature), 1994
Montreux – three holes	Reno, NV	Jack Nicklaus (Signature), 2001
Montreux Golf & Country Club	Reno, NV	Jack Nicklaus (Signature), 1997
Mount Juliet	County Kilkenny, Ireland	Jack Nicklaus (Signature), 1991
Muirfield Village Golf Club	Dublin, OH	Jack Nicklaus, Desmond Muirhead, 1974
Nanhu Country Club	Guangzhou, Guangdong, China	Jack Nicklaus (Signature), 1998
National Golf Club	Southern Pines, NC	Jack Nicklaus (Signature), 1989
Natural Park Ramindra Golf Club	Bangkok, Thailand	Jack Nicklaus (Signature), 1992
New Albany Country Club	New Albany, OH	Jack Nicklaus (Signature), 1992
New Capital Golf Club	Yamaoka, Gifu, Japan	Jack Nicklaus (Signature), 1999
New Saint Andrews Golf Club	Otawara, Tochigi, Japan	Jack Nicklaus, Desmond Muirhead, 1973
Nicklaus North Golf Course	Whistler, British Columbia, Canada	Jack Nicklaus (Signature), 1996
Oakmont Golf Club	Yamazoe, Nara, Japan	Jack Nicklaus (Signature), 1990
Ocean Hammock	Palm Coast, FL	Jack Nicklaus (Signature), 2000
Okanagan Golf Club – Bear	Kelowna, British Columbia, Canada	Bill O'Leary, 1999
Old Works Golf Course	Anaconda, MT	Jack Nicklaus (Signature), 1997
Olympic Staff Ashikaga Golf Course	Ashikaga, Tochigi Japan	Jack Nicklaus, Jack Nicklaus II, 2001
Palm Island Golf Club – Mountain and Arroyo Nines	Huiyang, Guangdong, China	Jack Nicklaus II, 1999
Palmilla Golf Club – Ocean Nine	San Jose del Cabo, Baja California Sur, Mexico	Jack Nicklaus (Signature), 1993
Palmilla Ocean Nine	San Jose del Cabo, Cabo San Lucas, Mexico	Jack Nicklaus (Signature), 1999
Paris International Golf Club	Paris, France	Jack Nicklaus (Signature), 1991
Park Meadows Country Club	Park City, UT	Jack Nicklaus (Signature), 1983
Pasadera Golf & Country Club	Monterey, CA	Jack Nicklaus (Signature), 2000
Pawleys Plantation	Pawleys Island, SC	Jack Nicklaus (Signature), 1988
Pebble Beach Golf Links – 5th Hole	Monterey, CA	Jack Nicklaus (Signature), 1998
Pecanwood	Bryanston, South Africa	Jack Nicklaus (Signature), 1998
PGA National – Champion Course	Palm Beach Gardens, FL	Jack Nicklaus, 1990 (Redesign)
PGA West – Private Course	La Quinta, CA	Jack Nicklaus (Signature), 1987
PGA West – Resort Course	La Quinta, CA	Jack Nicklaus (Signature), 1987

CLUB NAME	LOCATION	DESIGNER/CO-DESIGNER/YEAR
Phoenix Park Golf Club	Seoul, South Korea	Jack Nicklaus (Signature), 1998
Pine Valley Golf and Country Club	Changping, Beijing, China	Jack Nicklaus (Signature), 2001
President Country Club	Tochigi, Tochigi, Japan	Jack Nicklaus (Signature), 1995
Ptarmigan Country Club	Fort Collins, CO	Jack Nicklaus (Signature), 1988
Reflection Bay Golf Club at Lake Las Vegas	Henderson, NV	Jack Nicklaus (Signature), 1998
Richland Country Club	Nashville, TN	Jack Nicklaus (Signature), 1988
Roaring Fork Club	Basalt, CO	Jack Nicklaus (Signature), 1999
Rocky Gap Lodge and Resort	Flintstone, MD	Jack Nicklaus (Signature), 1999
Rokko Kokusai	Kobe, Hyogo, Japan	Jack Nicklaus II, 1996
Ruby Hill Golf Club	Pleasanton, CA	Jack Nicklaus (Signature), 1996
Ruitoque Country Club	Bucaramanga, Colombia	Nicklaus Design, 1997
Sailfish Point	Stuart, FL	Jack Nicklaus (Signature), 1981
Salem Glen Country Club	Cummons, NC	Nicklaus Design, 1997
Sanyo Golf Club	Okayama, Japan	Jack Nicklaus II, 1995 (Redesign)
Sendai Minami Golf Club	Shibata-gun, Miyagi, Japan	Jack Nicklaus (Signature), 1993
Shanghai Links	Pudong New Area, Shanghai, China	Jack Nicklaus (Signature), 1999
Sherwood Country Club	Thousand Oaks, CA	Jack Nicklaus (Signature), 1989
Sherwood Hills Golf and Country Club	Trece Martires, Cavite, The Philippines	Jack Nicklaus, Jack Nicklaus II, 1998
Shimonoseki Golden Golf Club	Yoshidachigata, Yamaguchi, Japan	Jack Nicklaus (Signature), 1989
Shoal Creek	Shoal Creek, AL	Jack Nicklaus (Signature), 1976
Shore Oaks Golf Club	Farmingdale, NJ	Nicklaus Design, 1989
Southshore at Lake Las Vegas	Henderson, NV	Jack Nicklaus (Signature), 1996
Spring City	Yiliang, Yunnan, China	Jack Nicklaus (Signature), 1997
Spring Creek Ranch	Collierville, TN	Jack Nicklaus (Signature), 1999
Springfield Royal Country Club of Cha-Am	Petchburi, Thailand	Jack Nicklaus (Signature), 1993
St. Andrew's Golf Club	Hastings-on-Hudson, NY	Jack Nicklaus, 1985 (Redesign)
St. Creek Golf Club	Asuke, Aichi, Japan	Jack Nicklaus (Signature), 1989
St. Mellion Hotel Golf & Country Club	Near Saltash, Cornwall, England	Jack Nicklaus (Signature), 1986
Stonewolf Golf Club	Fairview Heights, IL	Jack Nicklaus (Signature), 1997
The Summit Course at Cordillera	Edwards, CO	Jack Nicklaus (Signature), 2001
Sun Belgravia	Nukata, Aichi, Japan	Jack Nicklaus (Signature), 1996
Sungai Long Golf & Country Club	Selangor, Malaysia	Jack Nicklaus (Signature), 1993

CLUB NAME	LOCATION	DESIGNER/CO-DESIGNER/YEAR
Sunny Field Golf Club	Gozenyama, Ibaraki, Japan	Jack Nicklaus (Signature), 1988
Superstition Mountain Golf & Country Club Lost Gold	Superstition Mountain, AZ	Jack Nicklaus, Jack Nicklaus II, 1999
Superstition Mountain Golf & CC Prospector	Superstition Mountain, AZ	Jack Nicklaus, Gary Nicklaus, 1998
Suzhou Sunrise Golf Club	Lumu Town, Suzhou, China	Jack Nicklaus (Signature), 1997
Sycamore Hills Golf Club	Fort Wayne, IN	Jack Nicklaus (Signature), 1989
The Taman Dayu Club	Pandaan, Pasurvan-Jawa, Timur, Indonesia	Jack Nicklaus (Signature), 1997
Tamarin Santana Golf Club	Batam, Riau Province, Indonesia	Jack Nicklaus (Signature), 1995
Top of the Rock	Ridgedale, MO	Jack Nicklaus (Signature), 1996
TPC Michigan	Dearborn, MI	Jack Nicklaus (Signature), 1990
TPC at Snoqualmie Ridge	Snoqualmie, WA	Jack Nicklaus (Signature), 1999
Turtle Point Golf Club	Kiawah Island, SC	Jack Nicklaus (Signature), 1981
Valhalla Golf Club	Louisville, KY	Jack Nicklaus (Signature), 1986
Vermont National Country Club	South Burlington, VT	Jack Nicklaus, Jack Nicklaus II, 1999
Vista Vallarta Golf Club	Puerto Vallarta, Jalisco, Mexico	Jack Nicklaus (Signature), 2001
Wabeek Country Club	Bloomfield Hills, MI	Jack Nicklaus, Pete Dye, 1972
Westlake Golf and Country Club	Hangzhou, Zhejiang, China	Jack Nicklaus (Signature), 1998
Whispering Pines Golf Club	Trinity, TX	Bill O'Leary, 2000
Williamsburg National	Williamsburg, VA	Nicklaus Design, 1995
Winghaven Country Club	O'Fallon, MO	Steve Nicklaus, 2000
WuYi Fountain Palm Golf Club	Jiangmen, Guangdong, China	Jack Nicklaus II, 2001
Wynstone Golf Club	North Barrington, IL	Jack Nicklaus (Signature), 1989

Acknowledgments

This book could not have been produced without the dedicated assistance and expertise of several employees and friends of The Nicklaus Companies. The authors would particularly like to thank Scott Tolley, Jim Mandeville, Michelle Irwin, Pam Miller, Andy O'Brien, Ken Bowden, Rose Garrido, Ed Etchells, and the entire staff of Nicklaus Design, especially Nancy Petteruti and Chris Cochran. Thanks as well to all the golf course owners and managers who were so generous with their time and resources. Photos were supplied by numerous photographers, including Phil Arnold, Aidan Bradley, Dick Durrance, Mike Klemme, and Phil Sheldon.

Thanks to Pete Dye and Alice Dye. The formidable husband-wife team was very thoughtful and helpful, not only in contributing the Foreword to this book, but in hunting up historical photographs as well. Many thanks to George Peper, who was an advocate for this book from the beginning, as well as to his wife, the talented Elizabeth Peper, whose elegant color paintings of individual holes and the Muirfield Village course add grace and insight to these pages.

We extend our gratitude to Harry N. Abrams, Inc., particularly our gracious editor, Margaret L. Kaplan, the ever-present and resourceful Deborah Aaronson, and art director Robert McKee. Thanks also to John K. Crowley, whose passion for this project was palpable. Laurie Platt Winfrey at Carousel Research in New York did a remarkable job of assembling photos from all over the world. Thanks as well to Kestrel Communications, for allowing Chris Millard the freedom to pursue this idea.

We would like to thank the one person in the universe who could keep all of these creative minds on the same page. Without Marilyn Keough's interest in this project, her attention to detail, and her marshalling of resources, this book would have been just another good idea.

Finally, a very special thanks to our wives, Barbara and Eileen.

Index

Editor: Margaret L. Kaplan
Designer: Robert McKee
Photo Research: Laurie Platt Winfrey, Carousel
Research, Inc.; John K. Crowley
Production Consultant: Shun Yamamoto

Library of Congress Cataloging-in-Publication Data

Nicklaus, Jack.
  Nicklaus by design : golf course strategy and
  architecture/ by Jack Nicklaus with Chris Millard.
      p. cm.
Includes index.
  1. Golf courses—Design and construction.
  2. Nicklaus, Jack.
  I. Millard, Chris. II. Title.
  GV975 .N53 2002
  712'.5—dc21
                              2002018227

Printed and bound in Hong Kong
10 9 8 7 6 5 4 3 2 1

Harry N. Abrams, Inc.
100 Fifth Avenue
New York, N.Y. 10011
www.abramsbooks.com

Abrams is a subsidiary of

Photo Credits

Phil Arnold/Golfscape: 26–27, 30–31, 32–33, 35, 38–39,
    40–41, 88, 94–95, 108–9, 114–15, 117, 118, 119 top,
    125, 128, 134–35, 138, 139, 140–41, 144, 145, 146,
    149, 150–51, 153, 154, 176
Courtesy Australian Golf Club: 43, 156, 157
Liz Ball/Positive Images: 217 (2) 2nd row
Aidan Bradley: 61, 64–65, 66, 92, 110–11, 161, 166, 169,
    170, 172–73, 199, 202–3
Mark Brown/Courtesy Colleton River Plantation: 121
Rob Brown/Miller Brown: 96–97, 179
Courtesy The Bull at Pinehurst Farms: 190
Courtesy Colleton River Plantation Golf Club: 72–73
Crandall & Crandall: 217 (bottom 4)
Joann Dost/Golf Editions: 56, 76, 113, 133, 200, 207
    (Courtesy © Pebble Beach Company)
Joann Dost/Courtesy Muirfield Village Golf Club:
    44–45, 46
Dick Durrance/Courtesy PGA Tour: 58–59,
    186–87, 259
Dick Durrance II: 4–5, 22–23, 24–25
Courtesy Pete Dye: 7, 19
Patrick Eagar/Phil Sheldon Golf Library: 87
Courtesy Ford Motor Company: 258 (2)
Courtesy Golf Club of Purchase: 57
Courtesy The Greenbrier: 36

John & Jeannine Henebry: jacket front, endpapers, 1,
    54–55, 82, 162–63, 164–65, 192, 204–5, 236–37
Karina Hoskyns/Phil Sheldon Golf Library: 194
Mike Klemme/Golfoto: 77, 104–5, 191
L.C. Lambrecht: 214–15
Courtesy Loxahatchee Golf Club: 229
Jim Mandeville/Nicklaus Design: 2–3, 50–51, 52–53, 53
    (2), 68–69, 84–85, 89, 102–3, 188–89, 223, 228,
    230–31, 234–35, 240, 242, 243, 244, 245, 246, 248,
    249 (2), 250–51, 252, 253, 254–55, 255, 256–57, 273,
    jacket back
Grover Matheny, 2000: 98–99
Courtesy Muirfield Village Golf Club: 16
Nicklaus Design: 62, 71, 80, 110, 119 bottom; 143, 147,
    212, 225 (2), 226, 227, 271, 273
Courtesy Nicklaus Museum: 11, 12, 158
Elizabeth Peper: 42, 67, 75 bottom, 115, 123, 130–31, 213
Montana Pritchard/PGA of America: 116
John Rector, Turf Seed, Inc.: 217 (top 2)
Phil Sandlin/AP Photo: 261
John Seltzer, Courtesy Muirfield Village Golf Club: 101
Phil Sheldon: 14–15, 74, 75, 78–79, 122–23, 193,
    196–97, 208, 210–11, 264–65, 266 (all)
Jerry Tobias: 270–71
USGA Record: 247